The Persecution and Assassination of

# Jean-Paul Marat

as Performed by the Inmates of the

## Asylum of Charenton

under the Direction of

# The Marquis de Sade

D0032211

# The Persecution and Assassination of Jean-Paul Marat as Performed by the Inmates of the Asylum of Charenton under the Direction of The Marquis de Sade

### a play by Peter Weiss

English version by Geoffrey Skelton
Verse adaptation by Adrian Mitchell
Introduction by Peter Brook
Music by Richard Peaslee

WAVELAND
PRESS, INC.

Prospect Heights, Illinois

For information about this book, contact:
Waveland Press, Inc.
P.O. Box 400
Prospect Heights, Illinois 60070
(847) 634-0081
www.waveland.com

Cover: *Marat/Sade* performed by the Maryland Stage Company, directed by Xerxes Mehta. Photo by Terry Cobb.

Originally published in German under the title *Die Verfolgung und Ermordung Jean Paul Marats Dargestellt Durch Die Schauspielgruppe des Hospizes zu Charenton Unter Anleitung des Herrn de Sade*, copyright © 1964 by Suhrkamp Verlag, Frankfurt am Main

All inquiries concerning the rights for professional or amateur stock production should be directed to
Joan Daves, 59 East 54 Street, New York, NY 10022

Copyright © 1965 by John Calder Ltd.
Copyright © 1981 by Atheneum
Published by arrangement with Scribner, an imprint of Simon & Schuster, Inc.
2002 reissued by Waveland Press, Inc.

ISBN 1-57766-231-8

*All rights reserved. No part of this book may be reproduced, stored in a retrieval system, or transmitted in any form or by any means without permission in writing from the publisher.*

Printed in the United States of America

7   6   5   4   3   2   1

What's the difference between a poor play and a good one? I think there's a very simple way of comparing them. A play in performance is a series of impressions; little dabs, one after another, fragments of information or feeling in a sequence which stir the audience's perceptions. A good play sends many such messages, often several at a time, often crowding, jostling, overlapping one another. The intelligence, the feelings, the memory, the imagination are all stirred. In a poor play, the impressions are well spaced out, they lope along in single file, and in the gaps the heart can sleep while the mind wanders to the day's annoyances and thoughts of dinner.

The whole problem of the theatre today is just this: how can we make plays dense in experience? Great philosophical novels are often far longer than thrillers, more content occupies more pages, but great plays and poor plays fill up evenings of pretty comparable length. Shakespeare seems better in performance than anyone else because he gives us more, moment for moment, for our money. This is due to his genius, but also to his technique. The possibilities of free verse on an open stage enabled him to cut the inessential detail and the irrelevant realistic action: in their place he could cram sounds and ideas, thoughts and images which make each instant into a stunning mobile.

Today we are searching for a twentieth-century technique that could give us the same freedom. For strange reasons, verse alone no longer does the trick: yet there is a device. Brecht invented it, a new device of quite incredible power. This is what has been uncouthly labelled 'alienation.' Alienation is the art of placing an action at a distance so that it can be judged objectively and so that it can be seen in relation to

*v*

CONCORDIA UNIVERSITY LIBRARY
PORTLAND, OR 97211

the world—or rather, worlds—around it. Peter Weiss's play is a great tribute to alienation and breaks important new ground. Brecht's use of 'distance' has long been considered in opposition to Artaud's conception of theatre as immediate and violent subjective experience. I have never believed this to be true. I believe that theatre, like life, is made up of the unbroken conflict between impressions and judgments—illusion and disillusion cohabit painfully and are inseparable. This is just what Weiss achieves. Starting with its title, everything about this play is designed to crack the spectator on the jaw, then douse him with ice-cold water, then force him to assess intelligently what has happened to him, then give him a kick in the balls, then bring him back to his senses again. It's not exactly Brecht and it's not Shakespeare either, but it's very Elizabethan and very much of our time.

Weiss not only uses total theatre, that time-honoured notion of getting all the elements of the stage to serve the play. His force is not only in the quantity of instruments he uses; it is above all in the jangle produced by the clash of styles. Everything is put in its place by its neighbour—the serious by the comic, the noble by the popular, the literary by the crude, the intellectual by the physical: the abstraction is vivified by the stage image, the violence illuminated by the cool flow of thought. The strands of meaning of the play pass to and fro through its structure and the result is a very complex form: like in Genet, it is a hall of mirrors or a corridor of echoes—and one must keep looking front and back all the time to reach the author's sense.

One of the London critics attacked the play on the ground that it was a fashionable mixture of all the best theatrical ingredients around—Brechtian—didactic—absurdist—Theatre of Cruelty. He said this to disparage but I repeat this as praise. Weiss saw the use of every one of these idioms and he saw that he needed them all. His assimilation was complete. An undigested set of influences leads to a blur: Weiss's play is strong, its central conception startlingly original, its silhouette sharp and unmistakeable. From our practical experience I can report that the force of the performance is directly related to the imaginative richness of the material: the imaginative richness is the consequence of the amount of levels that are working simultaneously: this simultaneity is the direct result of Weiss's daring combination of so many contradictory techniques.

Is the play political? Weiss says it is Marxist and this has been much discussed. Certainly it is not polemical in the sense that it does not prove a case nor draw a moral. Certainly, its prismatic structure is such that the last line is not the place to search for the summing-up idea. The idea of the play is the play itself, and this cannot be resolved in a simple slogan. It is firmly on the side of revolutionary change. But it is painfully aware of all the elements in a violent human situation and it presents these to the audience in the form of a painful question.

'The important thing is to pull yourself up by your own hair To turn yourself inside out and see the whole world with fresh eyes.'

—Marat

How? someone is bound to ask. Weiss wisely refuses to tell. He forces us to relate opposites and face contradictions. He leaves us raw. He searches for meaning instead of defining one and puts the responsibility of finding the answers back where it properly belongs. Off the dramatist and onto ourselves.

LONDON                                                    PETER BROOK
1964

MARQUIS DE SADE *Sixty-eight years old, extremely corpulent, grey hair, smooth complexion. He moves heavily, breathes at times with difficulty, as if asthmatic. His clothing is of good quality, but worn. He is wearing white breeches with bows, a wide-sleeved white shirt with ornamental front and lace cuffs and white buckled shoes.*

JEAN-PAUL MARAT *In his fiftieth year, suffering from a skin disease. He is draped in a white cloth and has a white bandage round his temples.*

SIMONNE EVRARD *Marat's mistress, of indeterminate age. The player of the role is wearing a hospital uniform, with an apron and a headcloth. Her posture is crooked, her movements odd and constrained. When she has nothing to do, she stands wringing a cloth in her hands. She seizes every opportunity to change Marat's bandage.*

CHARLOTTE CORDAY *Aged twenty-four. Her clothing consists of a thin white blouse of Empire cut. The blouse does not conceal the bosom, but she wears a flimsy white cloth over it.*
*Her long auburn hair hangs down on the right side of her neck. She wears pink leather boots with high heels, and*

*when she is 'on stage' a ribboned hat is tied to her.*

*She is attended throughout by two Sisters, who support her, comb her hair and arrange her clothes. She moves like a somnambulist.*

DUPERRET      *Girondist Deputy.*

*The player of the role wears, in addition to his hospital shirt, a short waistcoat and the smooth tight trousers of an 'Incroyable.' His clothing is also white, with some ornamentation. He is held in the mental home as an erotomaniac, and takes advantage of his role as Corday's lover at every suitable opportunity.*

JACQUES ROUX      *Former priest, radical Socialist.*

*He wears a white hospital shirt with an overall shaped like a monk's robe. The sleeves of his shirt are tied together in front of him over his hands, and he can move only in the limits of this straitjacket.*

THE FOUR SINGERS    *Part crowd types, part comedians. They*
KOKOL, *Bass*      *have decked out their hospital uniforms*
POLPOCH, *Baritone*    *with grotesque bits of costume and wear*
CUCURUCU, *Tenor*    *the cap of the Revolution. Rossignol,*
ROSSIGNOL, *Soprano*   *with her tricolour sash and sabre, represents the figure of Marianne. They have singing voices and perform in mime.*

PATIENTS      *As extras, voices, mimes and chorus. According to need they appear either in their white hospital uniforms or in primitive costumes with strong colour contrasts. Any not required in the play devote themselves to physical exercises. Their presence must set the atmosphere behind the acting area. They make habitual movements, turn in circles, hop, mutter to themselves, wail, scream and so on.*

HERALD
*Wears a harlequin smock over his hospital shirt. His two-pointed cap is hung with bells and spangles. He is draped with numerous instruments with which he can make a noise as necessary.*
*He holds in his hand a beribboned staff.*

FIVE MUSICIANS
*Inmates of the mental home, clad in white. They play harmonium, lute, flute, trumpet and drums.*

MALE NURSES
*In light grey uniforms with long white aprons which give them the appearance of butchers. They carry batons in the pockets of their aprons.*

SISTERS
*Also dressed in light grey, with long white aprons, starched collars and large white bonnets. They carry rosaries. The Sisters are played by athletic-looking men.*

COULMIER
*Director of the mental home, in elegant light grey clothing, with coat and top hat. He wears pince-nez and carries a walking stick. He likes to adopt a Napoleonic pose.*

COULMIER'S WIFE AND DAUGHTER
*Form a composite pattern of colour from pale mauve to pearl grey, sprinkled with jewels and glittering silver.*

THE PERSECUTION AND ASSASSINATION OF
JEAN-PAUL MARAT
AS PERFORMED BY THE INMATES OF THE ASYLUM OF
CHARENTON
UNDER THE DIRECTION OF
THE MARQUIS DE SADE

# ACT ONE

*The asylum bell rings behind the stage. The curtain rises.*

1. ASSEMBLY

*The stage shows the bath hall of the asylum. To right and
left bathtubs and showers. Against the back wall a many-
tiered platform with benches and massage tables. In the
middle area of the stage benches are placed for the actors,
sisters and male nurses. The walls are covered with white
tiles to a height of about ten feet. There are window open-
ings high up in the side walls. There is a metal framework
in front of the platform and around the baths at the sides.
Curtains are fixed to each side of the framework before
the platform and these can be pulled when the patients
are to be hidden. Front stage centre there is a circular
arena. To the right of it a dais for MARAT's bath, to the
left a dais for SADE's chair. Left front a raised tribunal for
COULMIER and his FAMILY. On another tribunal right
front the musicians stand ready.*

*SADE is occupied with last-minute preparations for the
entry of the actors.*

*The MALE NURSES are completing a few routine opera-
tions of bathing and massage. Patients are sitting or lying
on the platform at the back.*

*SADE gives a sign. Through a side door at right back the
actors enter, led by COULMIER and his family and escorted
by SISTERS and MALE NURSES.*

*The PATIENTS rise to their feet.*

*The ceremonious procession comes forward. The asylum
bell is still tolling.*

3

MARAT, *wrapped in a white sheet and accompanied by*
SIMONNE, *is led to the bath.*
CORDAY, *sunk into herself, is taken to a bench by two sis-*
*ters.*
DUPERRET, ROUX *and the* FOUR SINGERS *take up their*
*positions as* COULMIER *reaches the stage. The* HERALD
*stands in the middle of the stage.* SADE *stands near his*
*raised chair. The tolling of the bell ceases.*
*The procession moves towards the acting area.*
COULMIER *enters the acting area.*
*The* PATIENTS *in the background stand tensely. One of*
*them adopts an eccentric pose, another comes slowly for-*
*ward with outstretched arms.*
*FANFARE.*

## 2. PROLOGUE

COULMIER:   As Director of the Clinic of Charenton
I would like to welcome you to this salon
To one of our residents a vote
of thanks is due Monsieur de Sade who wrote
and has produced this play for your delectation
and for our patients' rehabilitation
We ask your kindly indulgence for
a cast never on stage before
coming to Charenton But each inmate
I can assure you will try to pull his weight
We're modern enlightened and we don't agree
with locking up patients We prefer therapy
through education and especially art
so that our hospital may play its part
faithfully following according to our lights
the Declaration of Human Rights
I agree with our author Monsieur de Sade
that his play set in our modern bath house
won't be marred

4

by all these instruments for mental and **phys-**
ical hygiene
Quite on the contrary they set the scene
For in Monsieur de Sade's play he has tried
to show how Jean-Paul Marat died
and how he waited in his bath before
Charlotte Corday came knocking at his door

3. PREPARATION

*HERALD knocks three times with his staff and gives the orchestra a sign.*
*Ceremonious music begins.*
*COULMIER moves to his FAMILY.*
*SADE mounts his dais.*
*MARAT is placed in his bath. SIMONNE puts his bandage straight.*
*The SISTERS arrange CORDAY's costume.*
*The GROUP assumes the pose of a heroic tableau.*

4. PRESENTATION

*The music stops.*
                    *[Herald knocks three times with his staff]*
HERALD:        Already seated in his place
                    here is Marat observe his face
                              *[points his staff at MARAT]*
                    Fifty years old and not yet dead
                    he wears a bandage around his head
                              *[points staff at bandage]*
                    His flesh burns it is yellow as cheese
                              *[points at his neck]*
                    because disfigured by a skin disease
                    And only water cooling every limb
                              *[points to bath]*
                    prevents his fever from consuming him

**5**

[MARAT *takes his pen and begins to write*]
To act this most important role we chose
a lucky paranoic one of those
who've made unprecedented strides since we
introduced them to hydrotherapy
The lady who is acting as his nurse
[*points at* SIMONNE. *She bends with a jerky movement over* MARAT, *loosens his bandage and puts on a new one*]
whose touch certainly makes him no worse
is Simonne Evrard not Charlotte Corday
Marat and Evrard united one day
They shared one vision of the just and true
and furthermore they shared her money too
Here's Charlotte Corday waiting for her entry
[*points to* CORDAY *who smoothes her clothes and ties her neckcloth*]
She comes from Caen her family landed gentry
Her dress is pretty shoes chic and you'll note
she readjusts the cloth around her throat
[*points at it.* CORDAY *adjusts it*]
Historians agree so it's not lewd in us
to say that she's phenomenally pulchritudinous
[*She draws herself up*]
Unfortunately the girl who plays the role here
has sleeping sickness also melancholia
Our hope must be for this afflicted soul
[*With closed eyes, she inclines her head far backwards*]
that she does not forget her role

*[with emphasis, turning to* CORDAY]
Ah here comes Monsieur Duperret
*[indicates* DUPERRET]
with silken hose and fresh toupee
To the Revolution's murderous insanity
he brings a touch of high urbanity
Though as a well-known Girondist
his name's upon Marat's black list
he's handsome cheerful full of zest
and needs more watching than the rest
> *[*DUPERRET *approaches* CORDAY, *pawing*
> *her furtively. The* HERALD *raps him on*
> *the hand with his staff. A* SISTER *pulls*
> *back* DUPERRET.]
Jailed for taking a radical view
of anything you can name the former priest
Jacques Roux
> *[indicates* ROUX *who pushes out his*
> *elbows and raises his head]*
Ally of Marat's revolution but
unfortunately the censor's cut
most of his rabble-rousing theme
Our moral guardians found it too extreme

ROUX:    Liberty
> *[opens his mouth and pushes his elbows*
> *out vigorously.*
> COULMIER *raises his forefinger threaten-*
> *ingly.]*

HERALD:    Ladies and gentlemen our players
are drawn from many social layers
> *[He waves his staff over the audience*
> *and the group of actors.]*
Our singers for example of these four
each must be classified as bottom drawer
But now they've left the alcoholic mists

of slums and gin cellars our vocalists
  [*points to the* FOUR SINGERS]
Cucurucu Polpoch Kokol
and on the streets no longer Rossignol
  [*Each named changes his pose with a
  studied bow,* ROSSIGNOL *curtsies.*]
Now meet this gentleman from high society
  [*points at* SADE *who turns his back on
  the public in a bored way*]
who under the lurid star of notoriety
came to live with us just five years ago
It's to his genius that we owe this show
The former Marquis Monsieur de Sade
whose books were banned his essays barred
while he's been persecuted and reviled
thrown into jail and for some years exiled
The introduction's over now the play
of Jean-Paul Marat can get under way
Tonight the date
is the thirteenth of July eighteen-o-eight
And on this night our cast intend
showing how fifteen years ago night without
  end
fell on that man that invalid
  [*points at* MARAT]
And you are going to see him bleed
  [*points at* MARAT'*s breast*]
and see this woman after careful thought
  [*points at* CORDAY]
take up the dagger and cut him short
Homage to Marat
  [*Music starts.* CORDAY *is led by the* SIS-
  TERS *from the arena to a bench in the
  background.* SIMONNE *seats herself on
  the edge of the dais behind* MARAT'*s*

*bath. SADE goes to his seat and sits down.
ROUX and DUPERRET withdraw to a
bench.]*
*[The FOUR SINGERS take their position
for the homage to MARAT.]*

## 5. HOMAGE TO MARAT

| | |
|---|---|
| KOKOL & POLPOCH: | *[Recitative]*<br>Four years after the Revolution<br>and the old king's execution<br>four years after remember how<br>those courtiers took their final bow |
| CHORUS: | *[singing in the background]*<br>String up every aristocrat<br>Out with the priests and let them live on their<br>fat |
| CUCURUCU & ROSSIGNOL: | *[Recitative]*<br>Four years after we started fighting<br>Marat keeps on with his writing<br>Four years after the Bastille fell<br>he still recalls the old battle yell |
| CHORUS: | *[singing in the background]*<br>Down with all of the ruling class<br>Throw all the generals out on their arse |
| ROUX: | Long live the Revolution<br>*[The FOUR SINGERS and other PATIENTS<br>form an adoring group around the bath.<br>A wreath of leaves is held up.]* |
| PATIENT: | *[in background]*<br>Marat we won't dig our own bloody graves |
| PATIENT: | *[in background]*<br>Marat we've got to be clothed and fed |
| PATIENT: | *[in background]*<br>Marat we're sick of working like slaves |
| PATIENT: | *[in background]* |

9

KOKOL: Marat we've got to have cheaper bread
[*indicating wreath*]
We crown you with these leaves Marat
because of the laurel shortage
The laurels all went to decorate
academics generals and heads of state
And their heads are enormous
> [*The wreath is placed on* MARAT's *head,
> he is lifted from the bath and carried on
> the shoulders of two patients.*]

CHORUS: Good old Marat
By your side we'll stand or fall
You're the only one that we can trust at all
> [MARAT *is carried around the arena.* SI-
> MONNE *walks beside him looking up to
> him anxiously. The* FOUR SINGERS *and
> the* PATIENTS *in the procession carry out
> studied gestures of homage.*]

ROSSIGNOL: [*naively, taking the play seriously*]
Don't scratch your scabs or they'll never get
any better

FOUR
SINGERS: [Song]
Four years he fought and he fought unafraid
sniffing down traitors by traitors betrayed
Marat in the courtroom Marat underground
sometimes the otter and sometimes the hound

Fighting all the gentry and fighting every
priest
businessman the bourgeois the military beast
Marat always ready to stifle every scheme
of the sons of the arse-licking dying regime

We've got new generals our leaders are new
They sit and they argue and all that they do

10

is sell their own colleagues and ride on their
   backs
and jail them and break them or give them all
   the axe

Screaming in language no man understands
of rights that we grabbed with our own bleeding hands
when we wiped out the bosses and stormed
   through the wall
of the prison they told us would outlast us all

CHORUS &
FOUR
SINGERS:
Marat we're poor and the poor stay poor
Marat don't make us wait any more
We want our rights and we don't care how
We want our revolution NOW

*[MARAT is ceremoniously placed back in
the bath. The wreath is taken from his
head.*

*SIMONNE busily changes his bandages
and rearranges the cloth about his shoulders. Music ends.*

*SADE sits unmoving, looking across the
stage with a mocking expression on his
face.]*

HERALD:
The Revolution came and went
and unrest was replaced by discontent

## 6. STIFLED UNREST

PATIENT:   We've got rights the right to starve
PATIENT:   We've got jobs waiting for work
PATIENT:   We're all brothers lousy and dirty
PATIENT:   We're all free and equal to die like dogs
ROSSIGNOL:   And now our lovely new leaders come
they give us banknotes which we're told
are money just as good as gold

but they're only good for wiping your bum

[COULMIER *jumps up from his seat*]

ROUX: [*in the middle of the stage*]

Who controls the markets

Who locks up the granaries

Who got the loot from the palaces

Who sits tight on the estates

that were going to be divided between the poor

[COULMIER *looks around. A* SISTER *pulls* ROUX *back*]

PATIENTS: [*in the background, and beating out the rhythm emphatically*]

Who keeps us prisoner

Who locks us in

We're all normal and we want our freedom

CHORUS: Freedom Freedom Freedom

[*The unrest grows*]

COULMIER: [*knocking with his stick on the railing*]

Monsieur de Sade

[SADE *takes no notice*]

It appears I must act as the voice of reason

What's going to happen when right at the start of the play

the patients are so disturbed

Please keep your production under control

Times have changed times are different

and these days we should take a subtler view of old grievances

[*The* PATIENTS *are pushed back by the* MALE NURSES.

*Some* SISTERS *place themselves in front of the* PATIENTS *and sing a tranquillizing litany.*]

## 7. CORDAY IS INTRODUCED

HERALD:

*[Midstage, CORDAY, who is sitting slumped down on the bench, is being prepared by the SISTERS for her entrance.]*
Here sits Marat the people's choice
dreaming and listening to his fever's voice
You see his hand curled round his pen
and the screams from the street are all forgotten
He stares at the map of France eyes marching from town to town
*[Points to the map, which MARAT rolls up]*
while you wait
*[Turns round. In the background a whispering begins and spreads.]*

CHORUS:

*[whispers]*
Corday Corday

HERALD:

while you wait for this woman to cut him down
*[Points with his staff to CORDAY.*
*Orchestra plays the Corday theme.]*

HERALD:

*[waiting for the SISTERS to complete their preparations]*
And none of us
And none of us
*[CORDAY is led forward by the SISTERS]*
And none of us can alter the fact do what we will
that she stands outside his door ready and poised to kill
*[he taps the floor three times with his staff.*
CORDAY *is put in position in the arena.*

                              *This all resembles a ritual act.*
                              *The music ends.*
                              *The* SISTERS *step back.*]
CORDAY:                       [*sleepily and hesitantly*]
                              Poor Marat in your bathtub
                              your body soaked saturated with poison
                                      [*waking up*]
                              Poison spurting from your hiding place
                              poisoning the people
                              arousing them to looting and murder
                              Marat
                              I have come
                              I
                              Charlotte Corday from Caen
                              where a huge army of liberation is massing
                              and Marat I come as the first of them Marat
                                      [*Pause. A chord on the lute leads in the*
                                      *musical accompaniment.*]
                              Once both of us saw the world must go
                              and change as we read in great Rousseau
                              but change meant one thing to you I see
                              and something quite different to me
                              The very same words we both have said
                              to give our ideals wings to spread
                                      but my way was true
                                      while for you
                              the highway led over mountains of dead

                              Once both of us spoke a single tongue
                              of brotherly love we sweetly sung
                              but love meant one thing to you I see
                              and something quite different to me
                              but now I'm aware that I was blind
                              and now I can see into your mind
                                      and so I say no
                                      and I go

14

to murder you Marat and free all mankind
[*Music ends.*
CORDAY *stands with her head bowed.*
*The* SISTERS *lead her back.*]


## 8. I AM THE REVOLUTION

MARAT:
[*tyrannically*]
Simonne Simonne
More cold water
Change my bandage
O this itching is unbearable
[SIMONNE *stands ready behind him and
carries out with maniacal movements her
rehearsed tasks. She changes his bandage,
fans him with the shoulder cloth and tips
a jug over the bath.*]

SIMONNE:
Jean-Paul don't scratch yourself
you'll tear your skin to shreds
give up writing Jean-Paul
it won't do any good

MARAT:
My call
My fourteenth of July call
to the people of France

SIMONNE:
Jean-Paul please be more careful
look how red the water's getting

MARAT:
And what's a bath full of blood
compared to the bloodbaths still to come
Once we thought a few hundred corpses would
be enough
then we saw thousands were still too few
and today we can't even count all the dead
Everywhere you look
everywhere
[MARAT *raises himself up in the bath.
The* FOUR SINGERS *stretched out on the*

*floor play cards, taking no notice of* Ma-
rat.]
There they are
Behind the walls
Up on the rooftops
Down in the cellars
Hypocrites
They wear the people's cap on their heads
but their underwear's embroidered with
   crowns
and if so much as a shop gets looted
they squeal
Beggars villains gutter rats
Simonne Simonne
my head's on fire
I can't breathe
There is a rioting mob inside me
Simonne
I am the Revolution
[Corday *is led forward by the* Sisters.]

## 9. CORDAY'S FIRST VISIT

[Herald *taps three times with his staff
on the floor and points at* Corday, *who
is led on to the arena.*
Duperret *follows* Corday *and remains
with bent knee at the edge of the arena.*
Simonne *stands between her and the
bath.*]

HERALD:   Corday's first visit
          [Orchestra *plays the* Corday *theme.*]
CORDAY:   I have come to speak to Citizen Marat
          I have an important message for him
          about the situation in Caen my home
          where his enemies are gathering

16

| | |
|---|---|
| SIMONNE: | We don't want any visitors |
| | We want a bit of peace |
| | If you've got anything to say to Marat |
| | put it in writing |
| CORDAY: | What I have to say cannot be said in writing |
| | I want to stand in front of him and look at him |
| | [*amorously*] |
| | I want to see his body tremble and his forehead bubble with sweat |
| | I want to thrust right between his ribs the dagger |
| | which I carry between my breasts |
| | [*obsessively*] |
| | I shall take the dagger in both hands |
| | and push it through his flesh |
| | and then I will hear |
| | [*approaches* MARAT] |
| | what he has got to say to me |
| | [*She stands directly in front of the bath.* |
| | *She raises dagger and is poised to strike.* |
| | SIMONNE *stands paralysed.* |
| | SADE *rises from his seat.*] |
| SADE: | Not yet Corday |
| | You have to come to his door three times |
| | [CORDAY *stops short, hides the dagger* |
| | *and withdraws to her bench.* |
| | *The* SISTERS *and* DUPERRET *follow her as* |
| | *she leaves.*] |

10. SONG AND MIME OF CORDAY'S ARRIVAL
    IN PARIS

[*As an accompaniment to the song,* PA-
TIENTS *come forward as mimes. They walk*
*singly around the arena. With simple dis-*

*guises they present types in the streets.*
*One is an 'Incroyable' another a 'Merveil-*
*leuse' or a banner-bearer, a salesman and*
*cutler, an acrobat or flower seller, and*
*there are also some prostitutes.*
CORDAY *circles the arena in the opposite*
*direction. She represents the country girl*
*who has come to town for the first time.*]

FOUR
SINGERS:
[*on the edge of the arena, to a musical ac-*
*companiment. Song*]
Charlotte Corday came to our town
heard the people talking saw the banners wave
Weariness had almost dragged her down
weariness had dragged her down

Charlotte Corday had to be brave
she could never stay at comfortable hotels
Had to find a man with knives to sell
had to find a man with knives

Charlotte Corday passed the pretty stores
Perfume and cosmetics powders and wigs
unguent for curing syphilis sores
unguent for curing your sores

She saw a dagger its handle was white
walked into the cutlery seller's door
When she saw the dagger the dagger was
    bright
Charlotte saw the dagger was bright

When the man asked her who is it for
it is common knowledge to each of you
Charlotte smiled and paid him his forty sous
Charlotte smiled and paid forty sous

18

[*Mime of the purchase of the knife.* COR-
DAY *chooses the dagger, takes it and pays.
She conceals the dagger under her neck-
cloth. The* SALESMAN *looks down her
bosom with an admiring gesture.*]
Charlotte Corday walked alone
Paris birds sang sugar calls
Charlotte walked down lanes of stone
through the haze from perfume stalls
Charlotte smelt the dead's gangrene
Heard the singing guillotine
[*The mime procession grows larger and
develops into a dance of death.
The* MUSIC *underlines the monotonous
rhythm.
Two* PATIENTS, *covered with a cloth, rep-
resent a horse. They pull a cart in which
stand the condemned receiving last rites
from a priest.
The* PATIENTS *accompanying the cart
make ecstatic and contorted movements.
Some are seized with convulsions and
throw themselves down in fits. One hears
stifled giggles and groans and the stamping of feet to music.*]
Don't soil your pretty little shoes
The gutter's deep and red
Climb up climb up and ride along with me
the tumbrel driver said

But she never said a word
never turned her head

Don't soil your pretty little pants
I only go one way

Climb up climb up and ride along with me
There's no gold coach today

But she never said a word
never turned her head

CORDAY: [*in front of the arena, turned to the public.
Behind her the stamping continues*]
What kind of town is this
The sun can hardly pierce the haze
not a haze made out of rain and fog
but steaming thick and hot
like the mist in a slaughterhouse
Why are they howling
What are they dragging through the streets
They carry stakes but what's impaled on those
    stakes
Why do they hop what are they dancing for
Why are they racked with laughter
Why do the children scream
What are those heaps they fight over
those heaps with eyes and mouths
What kind of town is this
hacked buttocks lying in the street
What are all these faces
        [*Behind her the dance of death takes
        place.
        The* FOUR SINGERS *join the dancers.
        The cart is turned into a place of execu-
        tion. Two* PATIENTS *represent the guil-
        lotine. The execution is prepared in grue-
        some detail.
        * CORDAY *sits slumped at the foremost
        edge of the arena.*]
Soon these faces will close around me
These eyes and mouths will call me to join
    them

[*The mime depicts the piercing and bursting of the fat belly of the priest. The condemned man leans across the execution block. His hands are sawn off.*]

11. DEATH'S TRIUMPH

MARAT:  [*speaking to the audience*]
Now it's happening and you can't stop it happening
The people used to suffer everything
now they take their revenge
You are watching that revenge
and you don't remember that you drove the people to it
Now you protest
but it's too late
to start crying over spilt blood
What is the blood of these aristocrats
compared with the blood the people shed for you
Many of them had their throats slit by your gangs
Many of them died more slowly in your workshops
[*The hands of the victim fall off. Howls. The executioners start sawing off his head.*]
So what is this sacrifice
compared with the sacrifices the people made to keep you fat
What are a few looted mansions
compared with their looted lives
You don't care
if the foreign armies with whom you're making secret deals
march in and massacre the people

You hope the people will be wiped out so you
    can flourish
and when they are wiped out not a muscle
    will twitch in your puffy bourgeois faces
which are now all twisted up with anger and
    disgust
    [COULMIER *rises. The head falls off. Tri-*
    *umphant screams. The* PATIENTS *play*
    *ball with the head.*]

COULMIER: Monsieur de Sade
we can't allow this
you really cannot call this education
It isn't making my patients any better
they're all becoming over-excited
After all we invited the public here
to show them that our patients
are not all social lepers
    [SADE *does not react. He gazes with a*
    *mocking smile across the stage and cues*
    *the* HERALD.]

HERALD: [*tapping his staff before* COULMIER *has fin-*
*ished speaking*]
We only show these people massacred
because this indisputably occurred
Please calmly watch these barbarous displays
which could not happen nowadays
The men of that time mostly now demised
were primitive we are more civilised
    [HERALD *points with his staff at the exe-*
    *cution scene.*
    *Trumpet call.*
    *Procession of nobles forms quickly, lining*
    *up for execution.*]

CORDAY: [*rising*]
Up there on the scaffold

you stand completely still and stare
farther than your executioners can see
That is how I will stand
when it's all over
[*she closes her eyes and appears to be sleeping*]

SADE: Look at them Marat
these men who once owned everything
See how they turn their defeat into victory
Now that their pleasures have been taken away
the guillotine saves them from endless boredom
Gaily they offer their heads as if for coronation
Is not that the pinnacle of perversion
[*The victims kneel in front of the execution block. SADE gestures to the whole group to retreat. The PATIENTS withdraw. The cart is taken away. CORDAY is led to her bench. A curtain is drawn to hide the PATIENTS.*]

## 12. CONVERSATION CONCERNING LIFE AND DEATH

[*Order is restored at the back.
The SISTERS murmur a short litany.*]

MARAT: [*speaking to SADE across the empty arena*]
I read in your books de Sade
in one of your immortal works
that the basis of all of life is death

SADE: Correct Marat
But man has given a false importance to death
Any animal plant or man who dies
adds to Nature's compost heap

becomes the manure without which
nothing could grow nothing could be created
Death is simply part of the process
Every death even the cruellest death
drowns in the total indifference of Nature
Nature herself would watch unmoved
if we destroyed the entire human race
    *[rising]*
I hate Nature
this passionless spectator this unbreakable ice-
    berg-face
that can bear everything
this goads us to greater and greater acts
    *[breathing heavily]*
Haven't we always beaten down those weaker
    than ourselves
Haven't we torn at their throats
with continuous villainy and lust
Haven't we experimented in our laboratories
before applying the final solution
Let me remind you of the execution of Da-
    miens
after his unsuccessful attempt to assassinate
Louis the Fifteenth (now deceased)
Remember how Damiens died
How gentle the guillotine is
compared with his torture
It lasted four hours while the crowd goggled
and Casanova at an upper window
felt under the skirts of the ladies watching
    *[pointing in the direction of the tribunal*
    *where* COULMIER *sits]*
His chest arms thighs and calves were slit
    open
Molten lead was poured into each slit

boiling oil they poured over him burning tar
wax sulphur
They burnt off his hands
tied ropes to his arms and legs
harnessed four horses to him and geed them
up
They pulled at him for an hour but they'd
never done it before
and he wouldn't come apart
until they sawed through his shoulders and
hips
So he lost the first arm then the second
and he watched what they did to him and
then turned to us
and shouted so everyone could understand
And when they tore off the first leg and then
the second leg
he still lived though his voice was getting
weak
and at the end he hung there a bloody torso
with a nodding head
just groaning and staring at the crucifix
which the father confessor was holding up to
him
   [*in the background a half-murmured litany is heard*]
That
was a festival with which
today's festivals can't compete
Even our inquisition gives us no pleasure
nowadays
Although we've only just started
there's no passion in our post-revolutionary
murders
Now they are all official

We condemn to death without emotion
and there's no singular personal death to be
    had
only an anonymous cheapened death
which we could dole out to entire nations
on a mathematical basis
until the time comes
for all life
to be extinguished

MARAT:    Citizen Marquis
you may have fought for us last September
when we dragged out of the gaols
the aristocrats who plotted against us
but you still talk like a grand seigneur
and what you call the indifference of Nature
is your own lack of compassion

SADE:    Compassion
Now Marat you are talking like an aristocrat
Compassion is the property of the privileged
    classes
When the pitier lowers himself
to give to a beggar
he throbs with contempt
To protect his riches he pretends to be moved
and his gift to the beggar amounts to no more
    than a kick [*lute chord*]
No Marat
no small emotions please
Your feelings were never petty
For you just as for me
only the most extreme actions matter

MARAT:    If I am extreme I am not extreme in the same
    way as you
Against Nature's silence I use action
In the vast indifference I invent a meaning

I don't watch unmoved I intervene
and say that this and this are wrong
and I work to alter them and improve them
The important thing
is to pull yourself up by your own hair
to turn yourself inside out
and see the whole world with fresh eyes

## 13.  MARAT'S LITURGY

[*The curtain is drawn open.*
PATIENTS *move forward and arrange
themselves in a closed group.*]

HERALD:    Marat's liturgy

MARAT:    Remember how it used to be
The kings were our dear fathers
under whose care we lived in peace
and their deeds were glorified
by official poets
Piously the simpleminded breadwinners
passed on the lesson to their children

CHORUS:    [*murmuring in the background as* MARAT
*continues*]
The kings are our dear fathers
under whose care we live in peace
The kings are our dear fathers
under whose care we live in peace

MARAT:    And the children repeated the lesson they believed it
as anyone believes
what they hear over and over again
[CHORUS *repeats*]
And over and over again the priests said
[*accompanied by chorus of* PATIENTS]
Our love embraces all mankind

of every colour race and creed
Our love is international universal
we are all brothers every one
    [*continuing alone*]
And the priests looked down into the pit of
    injustice
and they turned their faces away and said
    [*accompanied by chorus of* PATIENTS]
Our kingdom is not as the kingdom of this
    world
Our life on earth is but a pilgrimage
The soul lives on humility and patience
    [*continuing alone*]
at the same time screwing from the poor their
    last centime
They settled down among their treasures
and ate and drank with princes
and to the starving they said
    [*accompanied by chorus of* PATIENTS]
Suffer
Suffer as he suffered on the cross
for it is the will of God
    [A *mime is performed.*
    PATIENTS *and the* FOUR SINGERS *come
    forward. Church dignitaries are depicted:*
    CUCURUCU *carries a cross made of brooms
    tied together and leads* POLPOCH *with a
    rope around his neck behind him.*
    KOKOL *swings a bucket as a censer.*
    ROSSIGNOL *counts her beads.*]
    [*Continuing alone*]
And anyone believes what they hear over and
    over again
so the poor instead of bread made do with a
    picture

of the bleeding scourged and nailed-up Christ
and prayed to that image of their helplessness
And the priests said
    *[Accompanied by chorus of* Patients.
    *The litanies of the* Sisters *can also be*
    *heard.]*
Raise your hands to heaven bend your knees
and bear your suffering without complaint
Pray for those who torture you
for prayer and blessing are the only stairways
which you can climb to Paradise
    *[speaking alone]*
And so they chained down the poor in their
    ignorance
so that they wouldn't stand up and fight their
    bosses
who ruled in the name of the lie of divine
    right

Chorus: Amen

Coulmier: *[rising and calling above the Amen]*
Monsieur de Sade
I must interrupt this argument
We agreed to make some cuts in this passage
After all nobody now objects to the church
since our emperor is surrounded by high-
    ranking clergy
and since it's been proved over and over again
that the poor need the spiritual comfort of the
    priests
There's no question of anyone being op-
    pressed
Quite on the contrary everything's done to
    relieve suffering
with clothing collections medical aid and soup
    kitchens

and in this very clinic we're dependent on the
  goodwill
not only of the temporal government
but even more on the goodness and under-
  standing of the church
HERALD:       [*raising his staff*]
If our performance causes aggravation
we hope you'll swallow down your indigna-
  tion
and please remember that we show
only those things which happened long ago
Remember things were very different then
of course today we're all God-fearing men
              [*makes the sign of the cross*]

## 14.  A REGRETTABLE INTERVENTION

              [A PATIENT, *a clergyman's collar round
              his neck, detaches himself from the group
              and hops forward on his knees.*]
PATIENT:      [*stammering incoherently*]
Pray pray
O pray to him
Our Satan which art in hell
thy kingdom come
thy will be done
on earth as it is in hell
forgive us our good deeds
and deliver us from holiness
Lead us
Lead us into temptation
for ever and ever
      Amen
      [COULMIER *has sprung to his feet.*
      MALE NURSES *throw themselves on the*
      PATIENT, *overpower him, put him under*

30

HERALD: [*swinging his rattle*]
The regrettable incident you've just seen
was unavoidable indeed foreseen
by our playwright who managed to compose
some extra lines in case the need arose
Please understand this man was once the very
well-thought-of abbot of a monastery
It should remind us all that as they say
God moves like man in a mysterious way
[*He swings his rattle.*
COULMIER *sits down.*
The PATIENTS *retreat and stretch out on the benches, supervised by the* SISTERS *and* MALE NURSES.]

## 15. CONTINUATION OF THE CONVERSATION BETWEEN MARAT AND SADE

SADE: Before deciding what is wrong and what is
right
first we must find out what we are
I
do not know myself
No sooner have I discovered something
than I begin to doubt it
and I have to destroy it again
What we do is just a shadow of what we want
to do
and the only truths we can point to
are the ever-changing truths of our own experience
I do not know if I am hangman or victim
for I imagine the most horrible tortures
and as I describe them I suffer them myself

31

There is nothing that I could not do and ev-
    erything fills me with horror
And I see that other people also
suddenly change themselves into strangers
and are driven to unpredictable acts
A little while ago I saw my tailor
a gentle cultured man who liked to talk philos-
    ophy
I saw him foam at the mouth
and raging and screaming attack with a cudgel
a man from Switzerland
a large man heavily armed
and destroy him utterly
and then I saw him
tear open the breast of the defeated man
saw him take out the still beating heart
and swallow it

> [A PATIENT, *in pacing across the stage,*
> *comes face to face with* COULMIER *and*
> *addresses part of his speech directly to*
> *him.*]

PATIENT:    A mad animal
Man's a mad animal
I'm a thousand years old and in my time
I've helped commit a million murders
The earth is spread
The earth is spread thick
with squashed human guts
We few survivors
We few survivors
walk over a quaking bog of corpses
always under our feet
every step we take
rotted bones ashes matted hair
under our feet

broken teeth skulls split open
A mad animal
I'm a mad animal
  [SADE *comes up to him and leads him
  gently to the back as he continues*]
Prisons don't help
Chains don't help
I escape
through all the walls
through all the shit and the splintered bones
You'll see it all one day
I'm not through yet
I have plans

MARAT: [*searches for his cue*]
HERALD: [*prompting*]
O this itching
MARAT: O this itching this itching [*hesitates*]
HERALD: [*prompting*]
This fever
MARAT: This fever beats in my head like a drum
my skin simmers and scorches
Simonne
Simonne dip the cloth in vinegar and water
cool my forehead
  [SIMONNE *hastens to him and goes
  through her motions.*]
SADE: Marat I know
that you'd give up your fame and all the love
  of the people
for a few days of health
You lie in your bath
as if you were in the pink water of the womb
You swim all huddled up
alone with your ideas about the world
which no longer fit the world outside

And why should you care about the world out-
　　side
For me the only reality is imagination
the world inside myself
The Revolution
no longer interests me

MARAT:　Wrong Sade wrong
No restless ideas
can break down the walls
I never believed the pen alone
could destroy institutions
However hard we try to bring in the new
it comes into being only
in the midst of clumsy deals
We're all so clogged with dead ideas
passed from generation to generation
that even the best of us
don't know the way out
We invented the Revolution
but we don't know how to run it
Look everyone wants to keep something from
　　the past
a souvenir of the old regime
　　　This man decides to keep a painting
　　　This one keeps his mistress
　　　This man keeps his horse
　　　He [pointing] keeps his garden
　　　He [pointing] keeps his estate
　　　He keeps his country house
　　　He keeps his factories
　　　This man couldn't part with his shipyards
　　　This one kept his army
　　　and that one keeps his king
And so we stand here
and write into the declaration of the rights of
　　man

**34**

the holy right of property
And now we find where that leads
Every man's equally free to fight
fraternally and with equal arms of course
Every man his own millionaire
Man against man group against group
in happy mutual robbery
    [*The* PATIENTS *stand up slowly, some*
    *step forward. The* SINGERS *take up their*
    *positions.*]
And ahead of them the great springtime of
    mankind
the budding of trade and the blossoming of
    industry
and one enormous financial upsurge
We stand here more oppressed than when we
    begun
    [*points across the auditorium*]
and they think that the revolution's been won

## 16.  THE PEOPLE'S REACTION

| | |
|---|---|
| THE FOUR SINGERS: | [*With musical accompaniment.*] |
| | Why do they have the gold |
| | Why do they have all the power |
| | Why do they have friends at the top |
| | Why do they have jobs at the top |
| | We've got nothing always had nothing |
| | nothing but holes and millions of them |
| KOKOL: | Living in holes |
| POLPOCH: | Dying in holes |
| CUCURUCU: | Holes in our bellies |
| ROSSIGNOL: | and holes in our clothes |
| THE FOUR SINGERS & CHORUS: | Marat we're poor and the poor stay poor |
| | Marat don't make us wait any more |
| | We want our rights and we don't care how |
| | We want our Revolution NOW |

HERALD: [*coming forward quickly, swinging his staff.
Music ends. The* FOUR SINGERS *and* CHORUS
*withdraw*]
Observe how easily a crowd turns mob
through ignorance of its wise ruler's job
Rather than bang an empty drum
of protest citizens be dumb
Work for and trust the powerful few
what's best for them is best for you
Ladies and gentlemen we'd like to see
people and government in harmony
a harmony which I should say
we've very nearly reached today
[DUPERRET *and the* SISTERS *busy themselves with* CORDAY, *who cannot be awak-
ened. They pull her to her feet and hold
her up and try to get her moving.*]

17. FIRST CONVERSATION BETWEEN CORDAY
AND DUPERRET

[CORDAY *is led forward by the two* SIS-
TERS, *supporting her under the arms.*
DUPERRET *walks behind, supporting* COR-
DAY'S *back with his hands.*]
HERALD: [*plays a few runs on his Pan-flute*]
And now nobility meets grace
Our author brings them face to face
The beautiful and brave Charlotte Corday
[*turns round in concern, nods in relief
and points his staff at* CORDAY]
The handsome Monsieur Duperret
[*With the help of the* SISTERS, CORDAY
*enters the arena.* DUPERRET *walks beside
her.*
*The* SISTERS *withdraw.*

36

CORDAY *and* DUPERRET *greet each other
with exaggerated ceremony.*]
In Caen where she spent the best years of her
  youth
in a convent devoted to the way of truth
Duperret's name she heard them recommend
as a most sympathetic helpful friend
  [DUPERRET *uses the scene to make amo-
  rous advances to* CORDAY.
  *The* HERALD *addresses* DUPERRET.]
Confine your passion to the lady's mind
Your love's platonic not the other kind
  [*He gives the* ORCHESTRA *a sign with his
  staff.* CORDAY *stands with head held back,
  eyes closed.*
  *The* ORCHESTRA *plays the Corday theme.*
  *The* HERALD *withdraws. He waits a few
  seconds and watches* CORDAY.]

CORDAY:     [*with her eyes closed*]
Ah dearest Duperret
  [*she hesitates then starts again as if sing-
  ing an aria*]
Ah dearest Duperret what can we do
How can we stop this dreadful calamity
In the streets everyone is saying
Marat's to be
  [*She hesitates.*
  DUPERRET *gently caresses her hips and
  back.*]
Marat's to be tribune and dictator
He still pretends that his iron grip
will relax as soon as the worst is over
But we know what Marat really wants
anarchy and confusion
  [CORDAY *stands sunk into herself.*]

37

DUPERRET:     [*embracing* CORDAY, *also as if singing an aria,*
              *but with great ardour*]
              Dearest Charlotte you must return
              return to your friends the pious nuns
              and live in prayer and contemplation
              You cannot fight
              the hard-faced enemies surrounding us
                   [*One of the* SISTERS *approaches* DUPER-
                   RET *and pulls back his hand, which he*
                   *had placed on her bosom.*
                   CORDAY *stands sunk into herself.*]
              You talk about Marat but who's this Marat
              A street salesman a funfair barker
              a layabout from Corsica sorry I mean Sardinia
              Marat the name sounds Jewish to me
              perhaps derived from the waters of Marah in
                   the Bible
              But who listens to him
              Only the mob down in the streets
              Up here Marat can be no danger to us
                   [DUPERRET *embraces* CORDAY's *hips.*
                   *The* FOUR SINGERS *are filling in time with*
                   *all sorts of pranks, throwing dice and*
                   *showing each other card tricks.*]
CORDAY:       [*suddenly awake and full of power*]
              Dearest Duperret you're trying to test me
              but I know what I must do
                   [*tries to free herself from* DUPERRET's]
                   *embrace. The two* SISTERS *standing be-*
                   *hind the podium interfere and pull back*
                   DUPERRET's *hands.*]
              Duperret go to Caen
              Barbaroux and Buzot are waiting for you
                   there
              Go now and travel quickly
              Do not wait till this evening

for this evening everything will be too late

DUPERRET: [*passionately, in aria style as before*]
Dearest Charlotte my place is here
[*throws himself on his knees and hugs her legs*]
How could I leave the city which holds you
Dearest Charlotte
my place is here
[*he forgets himself and becomes wilder in his embracing. The* HERALD *pushes him with his staff and then taps on the floor.*]

HERALD: [*prompting*]
And why should I run

DUPERRET: And why should I run
now when it can't last much longer
[*stroking* CORDAY *vigorously*]
Already the English lie off Dunkirk and Toulon
The Prussians

HERALD: [*prompting*]
The Spaniards

DUPERRET: The Spaniards have occupied Roussillon
Paris

HERALD: [*prompting*]
Mayence

DUPERRET: Mayence is surrounded by the Prussians
Condé and Valenciennes have fallen to the English

HERALD: [*correcting*]
Austrians

DUPERRET: To the Austrians
The Vendée is up in arms
[*with much ardour and vigorous embraces*]
They can't hold out much longer

these fanatical upstarts
with no vision and no culture
They can't hold out much longer
No dear Charlotte here I stay
    [*snuggles up to her and puts his head
    into her lap*]
waiting for the promised day
when with Marat's mob interred
France once more speaks the forbidden word
Freedom
    [DUPERRET *raises himself, clinging to*
    CORDAY, *tries to kiss her.*
    CORDAY *extricates herself, the two* SIS-
    TERS *come to her aid, pushing* DUPERRET
    *away and pulling her back to her bench.*
    *The* MUSIC *ends.*]

18. SADE TURNS HIS BACK ON ALL THE
    NATIONS

SADE:    [*shouting to* MARAT]
    You hear that Marat
    Freedom
    They all say they want what's best for France
    My patriotism's bigger than yours
    They're all ready to die for the honour of
        France
    Radical or moderate
    they're all after the taste of blood
        [*rising*]
    The luke-warm liberals and the angry radicals
    all believe in the greatness of France
    Marat
    can't you see this patriotism is lunacy
    Long ago I left heroics to the heroes
    and I care no more for this country

|  |  |
|---|---|
| | than for any other country |
| COULMIER: | [calling over them with raised forefinger] |
| | Take care |
| PATIENT: | [in the background] |
| | Long live Napoleon and the nation |
| | [a shrill laugh in the background] |
| KOKOL: | [at back calling] |
| | Long live all emperors kings bishops and popes |
| | [signs of disorder in the background] |
| POLPOCH: | Long live watery broth and the straitjacket |
| ROSSIGNOL: | Long live Marat |
| ROUX: | Long live the Revolution |
| | [shouting above the disorder] |
| SADE: | It's easy to get mass movements going |
| | movements that move in vicious circles |
| | [Shrill whistles in background. |
| | A PATIENT begins to run in a circle, a second and third join in. |
| | MALE NURSES pursue them and halt them.] |
| SADE: | I don't believe in idealists |
| | who charge down blind alleys |
| | I don't believe in any of the sacrifices |
| | that have been made for any cause |
| | I believe only in myself |
| MARAT: | [turning violently to SADE] |
| | I believe only in that thing which you betray |
| | We've overthrown our wealthy rabble of rulers |
| | disarmed many of them though |
| | many escaped |
| | But now those rulers have been replaced by others |
| | who used to carry torches and banners with us |
| | and now long for the good old days |

41

It becomes clear
that the Revolution was fought
for merchants and shopkeepers
the bourgeoisie
a new victorious class
and underneath them
ourselves
who always lose the lottery

FOUR
SINGERS:
Those fat monkeys covered in banknotes
have champagne and brandy on tap
They're up to their eyeballs in franc notes
We're up to our noses in crap

Those gorilla-mouthed fakers
are longing to see us all rot
The gentry may lose a few acres
but we lose the little we've got

Revolution it's more like a ruin
They're all stuffed with glorious food
They think about nothing but screwing
but we are the ones who get screwed

## 19. FIRST RABBLE-ROUSING OF JACQUES ROUX

ROUX:
[*springing on a bench in background, shouting*]
Pick up your arms
Fight for your rights
Grab what you need and grab it now
or wait a hundred years
and see what the authorities arrange
[PATIENTS *approach* ROUX *from the tribunal*]
Up there they despise you
because you never had the cash

42

to learn to read and write
You're good enough for the dirty work of the
    Revolution
but they screw their noses up at you
because your sweat stinks
You have to sit way down there
so they won't have to see you
And down there
in ignorance and stink
you're allowed to do your bit
towards bringing in the golden age
in which you'll all do the same old dirty work
Up there in the sunlight
their poets sing
about the power of life
and the expensive rooms in which they scheme
are hung with exquisite paintings
So stand up
Defend yourselves from their whips
Stand up stand in front of them
and let them see how many of you there are
        [*The* FOUR SINGERS *sit down in the arena*
        *and pass a bottle around.*
        *The two* SISTERS *grab* ROUX *from behind*
        *and pull him down from the dais.*]

COULMIER:   [*springing up*]
Do we have to listen to this sort of thing
We're citizens of a new enlightened age
We're all revolutionaries nowadays
but this is plain treachery we can't allow it

HERALD:     [*sounding a shrill whistle*]
The cleric you've been listening to
is that notorious priest Jacques Roux
        [*points with his staff at* ROUX]
who to adopt the new religious fashion

has quit the pulpit and with earthier passion
rages from soapboxes A well-trained priest
his rhetoric is slick to say the least
'If you'd make paradise your only chance
is not to build on clouds but solid France'
The mob eats from his hand while Roux
knows what he wants but not what he should
    do
Talk's cheap The price of action is colossal
so Roux decides to be the chief apostle
of Jean-Paul Marat Seems good policy
since Marat's heading straight for Calvary
and crucifixion all good Christians know
is the most sympathetic way to go

ROUX:    [*frees himself and jumps forward*]
We demand
the opening of the granaries to feed the poor
We demand
the public ownership of workshops and fac-
    tories
      [*The* FOUR SINGERS *listen to the disturb-
      ance, but soon lose interest. They quarrel
      for the last drop of the bottle.*]
We demand
the conversion of the churches into schools
so that now at last something useful can be
    taught in them
      [COULMIER *wrings his hands and signifies
      protest*]
We demand that everyone should do all they
    can
to put an end to war
This damned war
which is run for the benefit of profiteers
and leads only to more wars

44

[COULMIER *runs across to* SADE *and
speaks to him, but* SADE *does not react.*]
We demand
that the people who started the war
should pay the cost of it
[*The* FOUR SINGERS *continue their an-
tics.*]
Once and for all
the idea of glorious victories
won by the glorious army
must be wiped out
Neither side is glorious
On either side they're just frightened men
    messing their pants
and they all want the same thing
Not to lie under the earth
but to walk upon it
without crutches

COULMIER:  [*shouting over him*]
This is outright defeatism
At this very moment our soldiers are laying
    down their lives
for the freedom of the world and for our
    freedom
        [*turning violently to* SADE]
This scene was cut

SADE:  [*calling out, without concerning himself with*
COULMIER'*s protest*]
Bravo Jacques Roux
I like your monk's habit
Nowadays it's best
to preach revolution
wearing a robe
        [ROUX *is overpowered by the two* NURSES
        *and dragged off.* DUPERRET *makes violent*

45

*passes at* CORDAY, *who remains impassive.*
*The* PATIENTS *come forward restlessly.*]

ROUX:          [*as he is being strapped to a bench*]
Marat
Your hour has come
Now Marat show yourself
Come out and lead the people
They are waiting for you
It must be now
For the Revolution
which burns up everything
in blinding brightness
will only last as long as a lightning flash

## 20.  MONSIEUR DE SADE IS WHIPPED

[ROUX *jumps up, the bench strapped to*
*his back. He is overpowered.*
*The* PATIENTS *are pushed back.*
SADE *comes slowly into the arena. He*
*speaks without bothering about the*
*noise.*]

SADE:          Marat
Today they need you because you are going
    to suffer for them
They need you and they honour the urn
    which holds your ashes
Tomorrow they will come back and smash
    that urn
and they will ask
Marat who was Marat
Marat
Now I will tell you
what I think of this revolution
which I helped to make
            [*It has become very quiet in the back-*
            *ground.*]

46

When I lay in the Bastille
my ideas were already formed
I sweated them out
under the blows of my own whip
out of hatred for myself
and the limitations of my mind
In prison I created in my mind
monstrous representatives of a dying class
who could only exercise their power
in spectacularly staged orgies
I recorded the mechanics of their atrocities
in the minutest detail
and brought out everything wicked and bru-
    tal
that lay inside me
In a criminal society
I dug the criminal out of myself
so I could understand him and so understand
the times we live in
My imaginary giants committed
desecrations and tortures
I committed them myself
and like them allowed myself to be bound
    and beaten
And even now I should like to take
this beauty here
        [*pointing to* CORDAY, *who is brought
        forward*]
who stands there so expectantly
and let her beat me
while I talk to you about the Revolution
        [*The* SISTERS *place* CORDAY *in the arena.*
        SADE *hands her a many-stranded whip. He
        tears off his shirt and offers his back to*
        CORDAY. *He stands facing the audience.*
        CORDAY *stands behind him. The* PA-

TIENTS *advance slowly from the background. The ladies on Coulmier's dais stand up expectantly.*]

At first I saw in the revolution a chance
for a tremendous outburst of revenge
an orgy greater than all my dreams
　　[CORDAY *slowly raises the whip and lashes him.* SADE *cowers.*]
But then I saw
when I sat in the courtroom myself
　　[*Whiplash.* SADE *gasps.*]
not as I had been before the accused
but as a judge
I couldn't bring myself
to deliver the prisoners to the hangman
　　[*Whiplash.*]
I did all I could to release them or let them
　　escape
I saw I wasn't capable of murder
　　[*Whiplash.* SADE *groans asthmatically.*]
although murder
was the final proof of my existence
and now
　　[*Whiplash. He gasps and groans.*]
the very thought of it
horrifies me
In September when I saw
the official sacking of the Carmelite Convent
I had to bend over in the courtyard
and vomit
　　[CORDAY *stops, herself breathing heavily.*]
as I saw my own prophecies coming true
　　[*He falls down on his knees.* CORDAY *stands before him.*]

48

and women running by
holding in their dripping hands
the severed genitals of men
    [CORDAY *flogs him again. He groans and*
    *falls forward.*]
And then in the next few months
    [*hindered by his asthma*]
as the tumbrels ran regularly to the scaffolds
and the blade dropped and was winched up
    and dropped again
    [*Whiplash.*]
all the meaning drained out of this revenge
It had become mechanical
    [*Another blow. He crumples.* CORDAY
    *stands very erect.*]
It was inhuman it was dull
and curiously technocratic
    [*Whiplash.*]
And now Marat
    [*Whiplash.* SADE *breathes heavily.*]
now I see where
this revolution is leading
    [CORDAY *stands breathlessly, holding the*
    *whip over* SADE. *The two* SISTERS *move*
    *forward and pull her back. She does not*
    *resist, dragging the whip behind her.*
    SADE *continues, lying on his knees.*]
To the withering of the individual man
and a slow merging into uniformity
to the death of choice
to self denial
to deadly weakness
in a state
which has no contact with individuals
but which is impregnable

So I turn away
I am one of those who has to be defeated
and from this defeat I want to seize
all I can get with my own strength
I step out of my place
and watch what happens
without joining in
observing
noting down my observations
and all around me
stillness
    *[pauses, breathing heavily]*
And when I vanish
I want all trace of my existence
to be wiped out
    *[He takes his shirt and returns to his chair, slowly dressing.]*

## 21. POOR OLD MARAT

MARAT:     *[bent forward, sunk into himself]*
Simonne Simonne
    *[staring as if blind]*
Why is it getting so dark
Give me a fresh cloth for my forehead
Put a new towel round my shoulders
I don't know
if I am freezing or burning to death
    *[SIMONNE stands ready and bends over him with her jerky movements, puts a hand to his brow, changes the cloths, fans him. The PATIENTS cower behind the arena.]*
Simonne
Fetch Bas so I can dictate my call
my call to the people of France

[SIMONNE *shakes her head in horror and puts a hand over her mouth.*]

Simonne
Where are my papers
I saw them only a moment ago
Why is it so dark

SIMONNE: [*pushing the papers lying on the board nearer*]
They're here can't you see Jean-Paul

MARAT: Where's the ink
Where's my pen

SIMONNE: [*indicating*]
Here's your pen Jean-Paul
and here's the ink
where it always is
That was only a cloud over the sun
or perhaps smoke
They are burning the corpses
[*The* ORCHESTRA *plays. The* FOUR SINGERS *come forward.*]

FOUR SINGERS: [*singing to music*]
Poor old Marat they hunt you down
The bloodhounds are sniffing all over the town
Just yesterday your printing press
was smashed Now they're asking your home address

Poor old Marat in you we trust
You work till your eyes turn as red as rust
but while you write they're on your track
The boots mount the staircase the door's flung back
[*together with* CHORUS]
Marat we're poor and the poor stay poor

Marat don't make us wait any more
We want our rights and we don't care how
We want our Revolution NOW
> [*Music Finale.* SINGERS *withdraw. The*
> PATIENTS *close the curtain.*]

## 22. SECOND CONVERSATION BETWEEN CORDAY AND DUPERRET

> [*The* SISTERS *and* DUPERRET *busy them-*
> *selves with* CORDAY. *Together they raise*
> *her up. The* SISTERS *arrange her clothes*
> *and tie on her hat. The* HERALD *comes*
> *forward and knocks his staff on the floor*
> *three times.*]

HERALD:   [*plays a few runs on his Pan-flute*]
Now that these painful matters have been
    clarified
let's turn and look upon the sunny side
Fever sores blows not one of them destroys
the universal rule of love's sweet joys
Anger and woe don't give a true reflection
of life there's also spiritual affection
Recall this couple and their love so pure
> [CORDAY *is led to the center by* SISTERS.
> DUPERRET *has his arm around her.*
> *The* HERALD *points his staff*]
she with her neatly-groomed coiffure
> [*points to it*]
and her face intriguingly pale and clear
> [*points to it*]
and her eyes ashine with the trace of a tear
> [*points to them*]
her lips sensual and ripe seeming to silently
    cry for protection
> [*points to them*]

52

and his embraces proving his affection
> [*Points to* DUPERRET, *who lifts* CORDAY's *foot and kisses her shoe, then covers her leg in kisses.* CORDAY *pushes him back.*]

See how he moves with natural grace
> [DUPERRET *loses his balance and, without grace, sits on his behind, but rises immediately and strikes a comic amorous pose before* CORDAY, *who turns her face from him in disgust.*]

and how his heart sprints on at passion's pace
> [*points to* DUPERRET's *breast*]

Let's gaze at the sweet blending of the strong and fair sex

before their heads fall off their necks
> [ORCHESTRA *plays* CORDAY *theme. She hesitates, looking for her words.*
> *The* HERALD *prompts her.*]

HERALD:    One day it will come to pass

CORDAY:    [*in the aria style*]
One day it will come to pass
Man will live in harmony with himself
and with his fellow-man

DUPERRET:    [*covers her hand and arm with kisses*]
One day it will come
> [*he strokes her hair, singing in the aria style*]

a society which will pool its energy
to defend and protect
each person for the possession of each person
and in which each individual
although united with all the others
> [*putting a hand under* CORDAY's *dress. She defends herself.*]

only obeys himself

and so stays free
[DUPERRET *tries to kiss* CORDAY's *mouth.*
*She avoids him.*]

CORDAY: A society
in which every man is trusted with the right
of governing himself himself

DUPERRET: [*holding* CORDAY *and embracing her vio-*
*lently*]
One day it will come
a constitution in which the natural inequali-
ties of man
[CORDAY *leans back.* DUPERRET *jumps*
*after her, continuing*]
are subject to a higher order
[*breathless*]
so that all
[*One of the* SISTERS *gets hold of* CORDAY
*and leads her back.* CORDAY *is placed in*
*a heroic pose.*]
however varied their physical and mental
powers may be
by agreement legally
get their fair share
[*He utters a sigh of relief, and then he*
*also falls into a suitable pose so that they*
*form a pleasant tableau.*]

## 23. THESE LIES THEY TELL

[MARAT *raises himself up.* CORDAY *is led*
*back by the* SISTERS. DUPERRET *follows*
*her.*]

MARAT: These lies they tell about the ideal state
The rich will never give away their property
of their own free will
And if by force of circumstances
they have to give up just a little

here and there
they do it only because they know
they'll soon win it back again
The rumour spreads
that the workers can soon expect higher wages
Why

> [*The head of a* PATIENT *appears from be-
> hind the curtain, which is opened from
> inside.*]

Because this raises production and increases
  demand
to fill the rich man's gold-chest
Don't imagine
that you can beat them without using force

> [*The* PATIENTS *rise one by one and ad-
> vance slowly, listening intently.*
> CORDAY *lies stretched out on the dais,*
> DUPERRET *leans over her.*]

Don't be deceived
when our Revolution has been finally
  stamped out
and they tell you
things are better now
Even if there's no poverty to be seen
because the poverty's been hidden
even if you ever got more wages
and could afford to buy
more of these new and useless goods
which these new industries foist on you
and even if it seems to you
that you never had so much
that is only the slogan of those
who still have much more than you

> [*The* PATIENTS *and* FOUR SINGERS *ad-
> vance slowly.*]

Don't be taken in

when they pat you paternally on the shoulder
and say
that there's no inequality worth speaking of
and no more reason
for fighting
[COULMIER *looks around, worried.*]
Because if you believe them
[*turns towards the audience*]
they will be completely in charge
in their marble homes and granite banks
from which they rob the people of the world
under the pretence of bringing them culture
[COULMIER *leaves the platform and hur-
ries towards* SADE. *He speaks to him.*
SADE *does not react.*]
Watch out
for as soon as it pleases them
they'll send you out
to protect their gold
in wars
[SADE *rises and moves to the arena.*]
whose weapons rapidly developed
by servile scientists
will become more and more deadly
until they can with a flick of a finger
tear a million of you to pieces

SADE:    Lying there
scratched and swollen
your brow burning
[COULMIER *nods with satisfaction and
returns to the platform.*]
in your world your bath
you still believe that justice is possible
you still believe all men are equal
Do you still believe that all occupations

are equally valuable equally satisfying
and that no man wants to be greater than the
    others
How does the old song go

24. SONG AND MIME OF THE GLORIFICATION
OF THE BENEFICIARY

[*The* FOUR SINGERS *perform a mime, in
which they illustrate the cash value of
all the things* SADE *names.*]

SADE: One always bakes the most delicate cakes
Two is the really superb masseur
Three sets your hair with exceptional flair
Four's brandy goes to the Emperor
Five knows each trick of advanced rhetoric
Six bred a beautiful brand-new rose
Seven can cook every dish in the book
And eight cuts you flawlessly elegant clothes
Do you think those eight would be happy
if each of them could climb so high
and no higher
before banging their heads on equality
if each could be only a small link
in a long and heavy chain
Do you still think it's possible
to unite mankind
when already you see how the few idealists
who did join together in the name of harmony
are now out of tune
and would like to kill each other over trifles

MARAT: [*raising himself*]
But they aren't trifles
They are matters of principle
and it's usual in a revolution
for the half-hearted and the fellow-travellers

to be dropped

> [*Mime ends.* MARAT *stands up in the bath.*]

We can't begin to build till we've burnt the
old building down
however dreadful that may seem to those
who lounge in make-believe contentment
wearing their scruples as protective clothing
Listen
Can you hear through the walls
how they plot and whisper

> [MARAT *gets out of the bath and stumbles around the arena as if about to faint. Some nurses seize him and put him back into the bath.*]

Do you see how they lurk everywhere
waiting for the chance to strike

THE FOUR
SINGERS:

> [*to music accompaniment, singly, speaking in conversational tones while promenading*]

What has gone wrong with
the men who are ruling
I'd like to know who
they think they are fooling
They told us that torture
was over and gone
but everyone knows
the same torture goes on
The king's gone away
The priests emigrating
The nobles are buried
so why are we waiting

## 25. CORDAY'S SECOND VISIT

> [CORDAY *is prepared by the* SISTERS, *who lead her forward.* DUPERRET *follows them.* MARAT *sits waiting in his bath.* SIMONNE *changes his cloths.* SADE *stands in front of his chair.* CORDAY *is placed on the arena in a pose. She holds up her hand as if about to knock. The* SISTERS *stand behind her ready to support her.* DUPERRET *sits down. The* FOUR SINGERS *stop in front of the musicians.*
>
> *The* HERALD *gives* CORDAY *a sign with his staff, she moves her hand as if knocking, and the* HERALD *knocks three times with his staff on the floor.*
>
> *The* ORCHESTRA *plays the* CORDAY *theme.*]

HERALD:
Now Charlotte Corday stands outside
Marat's front door the second time she's tried
> [*points to* CORDAY. SIMONNE *straightens and goes a few steps towards* CORDAY.]

CORDAY:
[*quietly*]
I have come
to deliver this letter
> [*draws a letter from her bodice*]
in which I ask again
to be received by Marat
> [*hesitates*]
I am unhappy
and therefore have a right to his aid
> [CORDAY *holds the letter out to* SIMONNE. SIMONNE, *confused, takes a step towards* CORDAY, *returns to the back and begins to change* MARAT'S *bandage.*]

59

CORDAY: [*repeating loudly*]
I have a right to his aid
> [*She stretches out her hand.* SIMONNE
> *wavers nervously about, then runs to*
> CORDAY *and snatches the letter from
> her.*]

MARAT: Who was that at the door Simonne
> [SIMONNE *hesitates in confusion be-
> tween* CORDAY *and* MARAT.]

HERALD: [*prompting*]
A girl from Caen with a letter
a petitioner
> [CORDAY *is now standing sunk into her-
> self.* DUPERRET *rises and puts his arm
> around her waist.*
> *The two* SISTERS *come up.* CORDAY *is led
> off.*]

SIMONNE: [*confused and angry*]
I won't let anyone in
They only bring us trouble
All these people with their convulsions and
 complaints
As if you had nothing better to do
than be their lawyer and doctor and confessor
> [*She tears the letter up and puts the
> pieces in her apron. She puts a fresh cloth
> around* MARAT's *shoulders.*]

SADE: [*goes into the arena and stops near the bath.
Musical accompaniment.*]
That's how it is Marat
That's how she sees your revolution
They have toothache
and their teeth should be pulled
> [*The* FOUR SINGERS *mime the characters
> in his speech. They mime very slowly,*

*with economical gestures illustrating suf-*
*fering.*]
Their soup's burnt
They shout for better soup
A woman finds her husband too short
she wants a taller one
A man finds his wife too skinny
he wants a plumper one
A man's shoes pinch
but his neighbour's shoes fit comfortably
A poet runs out of poetry
and desperately gropes for new images
For hours an angler casts his line
Why aren't the fish biting
And so they join the revolution
thinking the revolution will give them every-
    thing
a fish
a poem
a new pair of shoes
a new wife
a new husband
and the best soup in the world
So they storm all the citadels
and there they are
and everything is just the same
no fish biting
verses botched
shoes pinching
a worn and stinking partner in bed
and the soup burnt
and all that heroism
which drove us down to the sewers
well we can talk about it to our grand-
    children

if we have any grandchildren
[MUSIC *changes to a quartet with tragic flavour.*]

THE FOUR
SINGERS:

[*taking up their positions*]
Marat Marat it's all in vain
You studied the body and probed the brain
In vain you spent your energies
for how can Marat cure his own disease

Marat Marat where is our path
or is it not visible from your bath
Your enemies are closing in
Without you the people can never win
[MARAT *lays himself wearily across the board.*]
Marat Marat can you explain
how once in the daylight your thought seemed plain
Has your affliction left you dumb
Your thoughts lie in shadows now night has come
[*The music changes to a dramatic growling.*
MARAT *is in a fever.* SIMONNE *feels his brow, fans him, changes his bandage.*]

## 26. THE FACES OF MARAT

[*The whole stage trembles and roars. The mimes appear with a cart. The cart is drawn by a man and a woman who represent* MARAT'*s parents. The characters in the cart stand for Science, the Army, the Church, the Nouveaux Riches. The priest blesses the owner of the sack of gold looted from the aristocrats. The fig-*

*ures are bedecked with medals and with*
*primitive insignia. The costumes are ex-*
*tremely grotesque.*]

MARAT: [*raising himself up*]
They are coming
Listen to them
and look carefully at
these gathering figures
Listen closely
Watch
Yes I hear you
all the voices I ever heard
Yes I see you
all the old faces
　　　　[*the loud noise continues*]

HERALD: [*tapping his staff*]
Ladies and gentlemen silence I pray
Let's hear what these people are aching to
　　say
　　　　[*pointing to figures*]
about this man
　　　　[*pointing to* MARAT]
whom they all understood
before they bury him for good
First the schoolmaster of that charming place
　　　　[*points to schoolmaster*]
in which this man
　　　　[*points to* MARAT]
spent his childhood days

SCHOOL-
MASTER: [*sings in a falsetto voice*]
Even as a child
this Marat
made groups of his friends
rush screaming at each other
they fought with wooden swords

*63*

but real blood flowed
[*cries are heard in the background*]
and they took prisoners
and bound and tortured them
and nobody knew why

HERALD: [*pointing to the figure representing* MARAT's *mother*]
Now let us hear this lady for she can
give us the inside story of this man
She smelt him from the very first
for from her womb young Marat burst

MOTHER: [*in a complaining voice*]
Wouldn't eat his food
Lay around for days saying nothing
Broke a lot of canes on his hide we did
[*she laughs shrilly. Laughter is heard in the background, also the sound of whipping.*]
Locked him up in the cellar of course
but nothing helped
There was no getting at him
Oh
[*she starts laughing again*]

FATHER: [*springing forward, in a hurried voice*]
When I bit him he bit back
his own father
Threw himself down when I wanted to hang him up
and when I spat at him he lay there stiff as a poker
cold as ice
[*starts to laugh harshly*]

MARAT: Yes I see you
hated father hated mother
[*The two figures squat down, still shak-*

64

*ing with laughter. They rock to and fro
as if sitting in a boat.*]
What's that boat you're rocking in
I see you
I hear you
Why do you laugh like executioners
[*The two figures sit rocking, their laughter dies.*]

SIMONNE: [*approaching the bath*]
Jean-Paul you're feverish
Stop writing Jean-Paul
or it'll kill you
Lie still
You must take more care of yourself

MARAT: I'm not feverish
Now I see clearly
those figures were always hallucinations
Why doesn't Bas come
Fetch him
My call to the nation
I must write my call
Bas

SCHOOL- [*jumping forward*]
MASTER: When he was five this loudmouth boasted
I can do anything teacher can do
and what's more I know more
and at fifteen I've conquered the uni-v-v-v-
versities
and outdone all the p-p-professors
and at the age of twenty I've mastered
the entire in-in-in-intellectual cosmos
That's what he boasted
as true as I stand here
[*swings his cane*]

MARAT: Simonne

|  |  |
|---|---|
|  | where are my old manuscripts |
|  | My novel about the young Count Potovsky |
|  | and my book about the chains of slavery |
| SIMONNE: | [*defensively*] |
|  | Leave all that stuff |
|  | It'll only bring you trouble |
| MARAT: | [*raising himself up*] |
|  | I want to see them |
|  | Look for them |
|  | bring them to me |
| SCHOOL-MASTER: | Scribblings of a pickpocket |
|  | pilfered thoughts |
|  | frivolities tirades |
| MILITARY REPRESENT-ATIVE: | One book published under the name of a count |
|  | The other under the name of a prince |
|  | Just look at him |
|  | this charlatan |
|  | greedy for titles and court distinctions |
|  | who turned on those he once flattered |
|  | only because they did not recognize him |
| A SCIENTIST: | What did he do in England this shady Marat |
|  | Wasn't he a dandy in the highest society |
|  | who had to run away |
|  | because he was caught red-handed embezzling and stealing |
|  | Didn't he smuggle himself back into well-known circles |
|  | and get himself appointed physician |
|  | to the Count d'Artois |
|  | or was it only to his horses |
|  | Didn't we see him going about with aristocrats |
|  | He charged thirty-six livres for a consultation |
|  | and on top of that enjoyed the favours of |

certain well-born ladies
>[COULMIER's *wife and daughter applaud.*]

A NEWLY
RICH:
And when at last they let him drop
back to his kind the simple poor
and when he spoke and couldn't stop
each word from branding him a boor
and when they found he was a quack
with watered drugs and pills of chalk
and when they threw him on his back
He raised his battered head to squawk
>Property is Robbery
>[*cries in the background*]
>Down with all Tyrants
>[*the cry is taken up in the background*]

MARAT:
Bas fetch Bas
>[VOLTAIRE *emerges from the darkness, suitably masked and with corkscrew curls.*]

CHORUS:
Bas

HERALD:
[*as* VOLTAIRE *advances*]
It is a privilege indeed
to introduce Voltaire He wrote Candide

VOLTAIRE:
[*monotonously*]
We have received from a certain Marat
a slim volume
entitled Man
This Marat claims in a somewhat revolutionary essay
that the soul exists in the walls of the brain
and from that strategic point controls
the hypodraulic mechanism of the body
by means of a network of tinkling nerve threads

67

At the same time apparently the soul is re-
    ceiving
messages from the mechanamism of the body
messages conveyed by pistons plugs and wires
which the soul transforms into consciousness
    through separate
centimentrifuges operating asimultaneously
In other words
it is the opinion of this gentleman
that a corn fills the corridors of the brain
    with pain of the soul
and that a troubled soul curdles the liver and
kidneys
For this kind of ring-a-ring-a-roses
we can spare not even our laughter
      [CUCURUCU *and* ROSSIGNOL *laugh ironi-*
      *cally Ha Ha Ha. A figure with a palm*
      *branch moves forward.*]

HERALD:    We're equally happy to welcome today
that eminent scientist Lavoisier
    [*points to him*]
LAVOISIER:    [*monotonously*]
The Academy has received from a certain
    Marat
some theories concerning fire light and elec-
    tricity
This Marat seems entirely certain
that he knows a great deal better than the
    Academy
For fire he says is not an element
but a liquid fluidium caused by heat
which only ignites because of air
Light he proceeds to say is not light
but a path of vibratorating rays
left behind by light

Certainly an extraordinary scientist
He goes further
Heat according to him is not of course heat
but simply more vibratoratory rays
which become heat only
when they collide with a body and set in mo-
tionability
its minuscule molecules
He wants to pronounce
the whole of firm and fixed creation
invalid
And instead he wants to introduce
a universe of unbridled activation
in which electrified magnetic forces
whizz about and rub against each other
No wonder that the author sits there in his
bath
attempting to determine the validity of the
proposition
The more you scratch the more you itch
[KOKOL *and* POLPOCH *laugh ironically*
*Ha Ha Ha.* FATHER *and* MOTHER *join in*
*the laughter. The figures mime the atti-*
*tude of judges about to give a verdict.*]

VOLTAIRE:       So this frustrated Newton's eyes
PRIEST:         turned to the streets He thought it best
SCHOOL-M:       to join the revolutionaries
NEWLY RICH:     and beat his dilettante breast
PRIEST:         crying out The oppressed must rise
LAVOISIER:      He meant of course I am oppressed
                [*Rocking to and fro and laughing, the*
                FATHER *and* MOTHER *pull back the cart*
                *with the figures.* ROUX *hurries to the*
                *front, a belated advocate.*]
ROUX:           Woe to the man who is different

**69**

who tries to break down all the barriers
Woe to the man
who tries to stretch the imagination of man
He shall be mocked he shall be scourged
by the blinkered guardians of morality
You wanted enlightenment and warmth
and so you studied light and heat
    [*unrest in background*]
You wondered how forces can be controlled
so you studied electricity
You wanted to know what man is for
so you asked yourself What is this soul
this dump for hollow ideals and mangled
    morals
You decided that the soul is in the brain
    [*The* PATIENTS *form into a group and ad-*
    *vance.*]
and that it can learn to think
For to you the soul is a practical thing
a tool for ruling and mastering life
And you came one day to the Revolution
because you saw the most important vision
That our circumstances must be changed
    fundamentally
and without these changes
everything we try to do must fail
    [COULMIER *jumps up. The* SISTERS *and*
    MALE NURSES *run towards* ROUX *and pull*
    *him into the background.* SADE *stands*
    *erect in front of his chair and smiles.*
    CORDAY *lies sleeping on her bench.* DU-
    PERRET *sits by her on the floor.*]

CHORUS:    [*to music while the* SISTERS *sing a litany*]
    Marat we're poor and the poor stay poor
    Marat don't make us wait any more

|            | We want our rights and we don't care how |
|            | We want our Revolution NOW [*music ends*] |
| HERALD:    | [*swinging his rattle*] |
|            | The end comes soon Before we watch the crime |

We want our rights and we don't care how
We want our Revolution NOW [*music ends*]

HERALD: [*swinging his rattle*]
The end comes soon Before we watch the
  crime
let's interpose a drinking thinking time
while you recall that what our cast presents
is simply this a series of events
but that our end which might seem prear-
  ranged
could be delayed or even changed
We will since it's a play not actual history
postpone it with an interval We guarantee
that after your refreshments and debating
you'll find Marat still in his bathtub waiting
    [*points to* MARAT]

CURTAIN

# ACT TWO

[*The handbell is rung behind the curtain. Curtain goes up.*]

### 27. THE NATIONAL ASSEMBLY

[*The setting is the same, but with the following changes:
DUPERRET sits on the steps leading to SADE's raised chair,
between the two PATIENTS representing prostitutes. On
the left are seated the PATIENTS who represent the Giron-
dists in the National Assembly.
SADE stands underneath COULMIER's platform. The bath
has been removed from MARAT's dais. On it are the FOUR
SINGERS and the PATIENTS who represent the Jacobites.
PATIENTS sit on benches alongside the arena. There are
more PATIENTS in the background listening. The entire
group composes a tableau. The bath, in which MARAT
stands, is wheeled in through the door at the back right.
CHORUS in sections:
A drawn-out cat-call.
A long monotonous whistle.
A muffled trampling of feet.
MARAT is pushed in his bath to the centre of the arena.
He stands straight and looks towards the HERALD.*]

HERALD:    Marat is still in his bathtub confined
but politicians crowd into his mind
He speaks to them his last polemic fight
to say who should be tribune. It is almost
night
        [*He gives the orchestra a sign with his
staff. A flourish. The people in the tab-*

leau spring to life, stamp their feet, whistle and shout.]

KOKOL: Down with Marat

CUCURUCU: Don't let him speak

ROSSIGNOL: Listen to him he's got the right to speak

POLPOCH: Long live Marat

KOKOL: Long live Robespierre

CUCURUCU: Long live Danton

MARAT: [addressing the audience. During his entire speech he never turns to those present on the stage. It is obvious that his speech is imaginary.]
Fellow citizens
members of the National Assembly
our country is in danger
From every corner of Europe armies invade us
led by profiteers
who want to strangle us
and already quarrel over the spoils
And what are we doing
[apathetic noises]
Our minister of war
whose integrity you never doubted
has sold the corn meant for our armies
for his own profit to foreign powers
and now it feeds the troops
who are invading us
[Cries and whistles.]

KOKOL: Lies

CUCURUCU: Throw him out

MARAT: The chief of our army Dumouriez

ROSSIGNOL: Bravo

POLPOCH: Long live Dumouriez

MARAT: against whom I've warned you continually
and whom you recently hailed as a hero

|  |  |
|---|---|
| | has gone over to the enemy |
| KOKOL: | Shame |
| ROSSIGNOL: | Bravo |
| CUCURUCU: | Liar |
| | [shuffling of feet] |
| MARAT: | Most of the generals |
| | who wear our uniform |
| | are sympathetic with the emigrés |
| | and when the emigrés return |
| | our generals will be out to welcome them |
| KOKOL: | Execute them |
| CUCURUCU: | Down with Marat |
| ROSSIGNOL: | Bravo |
| POLPOCH: | Long live Marat |
| MARAT: | Our trusted minister of finance |
| | the celebrated Monsieur Cambon |
| | is issuing fake banknotes thus increasing infla- |
| | tion |
| | and diverting a fortune into his own pocket |
| | [whistles and stamping] |
| ROSSIGNOL: | Long live free enterprise |
| MARAT: | And I am told |
| | that Perregeaux our most intelligent banker |
| | is in league with the English |
| | and in his armoured vaults |
| | is organising a centre of espionage against us |
| COULMIER: | [jumping up to protest] |
| | That's enough |
| | We're living in eighteen hundred and eight |
| | and the names which were dragged through |
| | the gutter then |
| | have been deservedly rehabilitated |
| | by the command of the Emperor |
| ROSSIGNOL: | Go on |
| KOKOL: | Shut up Marat |

| | |
|---|---|
| CUCURUCU: | Shut his mouth |
| POLPOCH: | Long live Marat |
| MARAT: | [*interrupting*] |
| | The people can't pay the inflated price of bread |
| | Our soldiers march in rags |
| | The counter-revolution has started a new civil war |
| | and what are we doing |
| | The farms we confiscated from the churches have so far produced nothing |
| | to feed the dispossessed |
| | and years have passed since I proposed these farms |
| | should be divided into allotments |
| | and given farm implements and seed |
| | And why have we seen no communal workshops |
| | which were to be started in the old monasteries and country houses |
| | Those who have jobs |
| | must sweat for agents stockbrokers and speculators |
| | [*wild cries*] |
| | Fellow citizens |
| | did we fight for the freedom of those |
| | who now exploit us again |
| KOKOL: | Sit down |
| ROSSIGNOL: | Hear hear |
| CUCURUCU: | Sit down |
| POLPOCH: | Hear hear |
| MARAT: | Our country is in danger |
| | We talk about France |
| | but who is France for |
| | We talk about freedom |

but who's this freedom for
Members of the National Assembly
you will never shake off the past
you'll never understand
the great upheaval in which you find yourselves
    [*whistles and cries of Boo*]
Why aren't there thousands of public seats
in this assembly
so anyone who wants
can hear what's being discussed

DUPERRET: What is he trying to do
He's trying to rouse the people again
Look who sits on the public benches
Knitting-women    concierges    and    washer-
    women
with no one to employ them any more
And who has he got on his side
Pickpockets layabouts parasites
who loiter in the boulevards
    [*indignation among the onlookers*]
and hang around the cafés

CUCURUCU: Wish we could

DUPERRET: Released prisoners
escaped lunatics
    [*tumult and whistling*]
Does he want to rule our country
with these

MARAT: You are liars
You hate the people
    [*cries of indignation*]

ROSSIGNOL: Well done Marat

POLPOCH: That's true

MARAT: You'll never stop talking of the people
as a rough and formless mass
Why

Because you live apart from them
You let yourselves be dragged into the Revolution
knowing nothing about its principles
Has not our respected Danton himself an-
nounced
that instead of banning riches
we should try
to make poverty respectable
And Robespierre
who turns white when the word force is used
doesn't he sit at high-class tables
making cultural conversation
by candlelight
  [*tongue clicking*]

KOKOL: Shame
CUCURUCU: Down with Robespierre
POLPOCH: Long live Marat
ROSSIGNOL: Down with Danton
MARAT: And you still long to ape them
those powdered chimpanzees
Necker Lafayette Talleyrand
COULMIER: [*interrupting*]
That's enough
If you use any more of these passages
we agreed to cut
I will stop your play
MARAT: [*breaking in*]
and all the rest of them
What we need now is a true deputy of the
people
one who's incorruptible
one we can trust
Things are breaking down things are chaotic
that is good

|  |  |
|---|---|
|  | that's the first step |
|  | Now we must take the next step |
|  | and choose a man |
|  | who will rule for you |
| ROSSIGNOL: | Marat for dictator |
| POLPOCH: | Marat in his bathtub |
| KOKOL: | Send him down the sewers |
| CUCURUCU: | Dictator of the rats |
| MARAT: | Dictator The word must be abolished |
|  | I hate anything to do with masters and slaves |
|  | I am talking about a leader |
|  | who in this hour of crisis |

      *[his words are drowned in the mighty*
      *tumult]*

|  |  |
|---|---|
| DUPERRET: | He's trying to incite them |
|  | to new murders |
| MARAT: | We do not murder |
|  | we kill in self-defence |
|  | We are fighting |
|  | for our lives |
| DUPERRET: | Oh if only we could have constructive thought |
|  | instead of agitation |
|  | If only beauty and concord could once more replace |
|  | hysteria and fanaticism |

      *[The* FOUR SINGERS *throw themselves on*
      DUPERRET *and stop his mouth.]*

|  |  |
|---|---|
| ROUX: | *[jumping up in the background]* |
|  | Look what's happening |
|  | Join together |
|  | Cast down your enemies |
|  | disarm them |
|  | For if they win |
|  | they will spare |
|  | not one of you |

and all that you have won so far
will be lost
> [*Enthusiastic calls, whistles and tram-
> pling.*]

CALLS: [*in spoken chorus, simultaneously*]
Marat Marat Marat Marat
Boo
A laurel wreath for Marat
Down with Marat
A victory parade for Marat
Down with him
Long live the streets
Long live the lamp-posts
Long live the bakers' shops
Long live freedom
> [*Disorder and screams. The* PATIENTS
> *tumble forward.* MARAT's *bath is pushed
> on to the platform right.*]

KOKOL & [*dancing*]
POLPOCH: Hit at the rich until they crash
Throw down their god and divide their cash

CUCURUCU & [*dancing*]
ROSSIGNOL: We wouldn't mind a tasty meal
of paté de foie and filleted eel

CHORUS: Marat Marat Marat Marat Marat
> [SADE *raises his hands. They all freeze.
> Roll of drums and beginning of music.*]

28. POOR MARAT IN YOUR BATHTUB SEAT

> [MARAT *sinks back into his bath. Ex-
> hausted, he leans forward on the board.
> The spectators' benches are pushed back,
> the* SISTERS *and* NURSES *force back the*
> PATIENTS. *In front of the arena the* FOUR
> SINGERS *dance a slow Carmagnole.*]

| | |
|---|---|
| FOUR SINGERS: | [*accompanied, singing and dancing*]<br>Poor Marat in your bathtub seat<br>your life on this planet is near complete<br>Closer and closer to you death creeps<br>though there on her bench Charlotte Corday<br>   sleeps<br><br>Poor Marat if she slept too late<br>while dreaming of fairy-tale heads of state<br>maybe your sickness would disappear<br>Charlotte Corday would not find you here<br><br>Poor Marat stay wide awake<br>and be on your guard for the people's sake<br>Stare through the failing evening light<br>for this is the evening before the night<br>     [*Drums. In the background order has<br>     been restored after a fashion. The PA-<br>     TIENTS should be standing upright, their<br>     hands crossed above their heads. SISTERS<br>     are standing before them, folding their<br>     hands and praying. The murmur of pray-<br>     ers can be heard. The FOUR SISTERS<br>     dance on a while and then stretch them-<br>     selves out on the arena before MARAT's<br>     bath.*] |
| MARAT: | [*with fear in his voice*]<br>What is that knocking Simonne<br>     [*tyrannic again*]<br>Simonne<br>more cold water<br>     [SIMONNE *sits huddled up at the edge of<br>     the platform and doesn't react.*]<br>Simonne<br>Where is Bas |

SADE:      Give up Marat
           You said yourself
           nothing can be achieved by scribbling
           Long ago I abandoned my masterpiece
           a roll of paper thirty yards long
           which I filled completely with minute hand-
               writing
           in my dungeon years ago
           It vanished when the Bastille fell
           it vanished as everything written
           everything thought and planned
           will disappear
               [MARAT *lies with his face on the board
               and covers his ears with his hands.*]

SADE:      [*continues*]
           Marat
           Look at me
           Marat can you call this living
           in your bath
           in your mortification
               [*By order of the* SISTERS *the* PATIENTS
               *change their position and stretch up their
               hands.*]

MARAT:     [*raising himself up*]
           I had time for nothing but work
           Day and night were not enough for me
           When I investigated a wrong it grew branches
           and every branch grew twigs
           Wherever I turned
           I found corruption
               [*A* PATIENT *falls over in the ranks. A*
               NURSE *carries him off.*]
           When I wrote
           I always wrote with action in mind
           kept sight of the fact

that writing was just a preparation
When I wrote
I always wrote in a fever
hearing the roar of action
When I was preparing
my book on the chains of slavery
I sat for three months
twenty-one hours a day
collecting material dreaming of material
paper piling high parchment crackling
until I sank into the swamps of overwork
That manuscript was suppressed
They were always ready
to pick up my statements
to slander them maim them
After each pamphlet was published
I had to go into hiding
They came with cannons
A thousand men of the National Guard
surrounded my house
And even today
I still wait for the knocking at the door
wait
for the bayonet to point at my breast
Simonne
Simonne
Fetch Bas
so that I can dictate my call
my fourteenth of July call

SADE:     Why all these calls to the nation
It's too late Marat
forget your call
it contains only lies
What do you still want from the revolution
Where is it going

Look at these lost revolutionaries
> [*Pointing to the* FOUR SINGERS *who lie
> stretched out on the floor, scratching
> themselves, yawning and trying to get the
> last drop out of the empty bottle.*]

What will you order them to do
Where will you lead them
> [*In the background the* PATIENTS, *on the*
> SISTERS' *command, must stand on one
> leg.*]

Once you attacked the authorities who turned
the law into instruments of oppression
Do you want someone to rule you
to control the words you write
and tell you
what work you must do
and repeat to you the new laws
over and over
until you can recite them in your sleep
> [*The* PATIENTS *in the background walk
> in a circle while the* SISTERS *pray. The*
> FOUR SINGERS *begin to hum unconcern-
> edly, lying at first on the floor with legs
> waving in the air. Then* ROSSIGNOL *and*
> CUCURUCU *get up and dance to the
> hummed melody.*]

MARAT: [*falling across the board again*]
Why is everything so confused now
Everything I wrote or spoke
was considered and true
each argument was sound
And now
doubt
Why does everything sound false
> [*singing and dancing*]

84

THE FOUR        Poor old Marat you lie prostrate
SINGERS:        while others are gambling with France's fate
                Your words have turned into a flood
                which covers all France with her people's
                blood
                        [*Music ends. The* FOUR SINGERS *dance
                        back to the centre of the stage. The* PA-
                        TIENTS *are led to their platform. The*
                        SISTERS *try to wake* CORDAY. *Loud knock-
                        ing three times.*]


## 29.  PREPARATIONS FOR THE THIRD VISIT

HERALD:         Corday
                wake up
                        [*Pause. The name* CORDAY *is whispered
                        in the background. The whispering swells
                        up and spreads over the whole stage. The*
                        SISTERS *shake* CORDAY, DUPERRET *calls
                        her name.* SIMONNE *stands awkwardly by
                        the bath and gazes across at* CORDAY.]

CHORUS:         Corday
                Corday
                Corday
HERALD:         [*signals to the orchestra with his staff*]
                Corday you have an appointment to keep
                and there is no more time for sleep
                Charlotte Corday awake and stand
                Take the dagger in your hand
                        [*Pause. The* SISTERS *raise* CORDAY *to her
                        feet.* CORDAY *stands with lowered head
                        and wobbly legs. The* SISTERS *support her
                        and lead her slowly forward. Her legs drag
                        along the floor.* DUPERRET *walks behind
                        her with his hands around her hips.*]

HERALD:     Come on Charlotte do your deed
            soon you'll get all the sleep you need
                    [CORDAY *is pushed into the arena. The*
                    *two* SISTERS *stand at her side holding her*
                    *firmly.* DUPERRET, *standing behind her,*
                    *supports her back. Music ends.*]
CORDAY:     [*her eyes still closed, speaking softly, nerv-*
            *ously*]
            Now I know what it is like
            when the head is cut off the body
            Oh this moment
            hands tied behind the back
            feet bound together
            neck bared
            hair cut off
            knees on the boards
            the head already laid
            in the metal slot
            looking down into the dripping basket
            The sound of the blade rising
            and from its slanting edge
            the blood still drops
            and then the downward slide
            to split us in two
                    [*pause*]
            They say
            that the head
            held high in the executioner's hand
            still lives
            that the eyes still see
            that the tongue still writhes
            and down below the arms and legs still shud-
                der
DUPERRET:   [*accompanied by lute. He is still holding his*
            *hand on her hip.*]

86

Charlotte awaken from your nightmare
Wake up Charlotte and look at the trees
look at the rose-coloured evening sky
in which your lovely bosom heaves
> [*Pause. He lifts his hand and strokes her
> on the bosom. He notices the dagger un-
> der the cloth.*]
Forget your worries abandon each care
and breathe in the warmth of the summer-
    time air
What are you hiding
A dagger
throw it away
> [*the music ends*]

CORDAY:       [*pushes his hand away*]
We should all carry weapons nowadays
in self-defence

DUPERRET:     [*beseechingly*]
No one will attack you Charlotte
Charlotte throw the dagger away
go away
go back to Caen

CORDAY:       [*drawing herself up and pushing the* SISTERS'
*hands away*]
In my room in Caen
on the table under the open window
lies open The Book of Judith
Dressed in her legendary beauty
she entered the tent of the enemy
and with a single blow
slew him

DUPERRET:     Charlotte
what are you planning

CORDAY:       [*forlorn again*]
Look at this city

Its prisons are crowded
with our friends
I was among them just now
in my sleep
They all stand huddled together there
and hear through the windows
the guards talking about executions
Now they talk of people as gardeners talk of
    leaves for burning
Their names are crossed off the top of a list
and as the list grows shorter
more names are added at the bottom
I stood with them
and we waited
for our own names to be called

DUPERRET:    Charlotte
let us leave together
this very evening

CORDAY:    [*as if she has not heard him*]
What kind of town is this
What sort of streets are these
Who invented this
who profits by it
I saw peddlers
at every corner
they're selling little guillotines
with tiny sharp blades
and dolls filled with red liquid
which spurts from the neck
when the sentence is carried out
What kind of children are these
who can play
with this toy so efficiently
and who is judging
who is judging

[PATIENTS *move to a group at centre.*
CORDAY *raises her hand to knock.*]

## 30. CORDAY'S THIRD AND LAST VISIT

[*The* HERALD *knocks three times on the
floor with his staff while* CORDAY *carries
out the knocking movement with her
hand.*
MARAT *starts up and looks in* CORDAY'*s
direction.*
SIMONNE *places herself protectively in
front of the bath.*]

DUPERRET: What do you want at this door
Do you know who lives here
CORDAY: The man
for whose sake I have come here
DUPERRET: What do you want from him
Turn back Charlotte
[*goes on his knees before her*]
CORDAY: I have a task
which I must carry out
Go
[*pushes him with her foot*]
leave me alone
[DUPERRET *embraces her legs. She kicks
out at him several times.* DUPERRET
*moves back on his knees.*]
HERALD: Now for the third time you observe
the girl whose job it is to serve
[*points to* CORDAY]
as Charlotte Corday stands once more
waiting outside Marat's door
Duperret you see before her languish
[*points to* DUPERRET]

prostrated by their parting's anguish
        [*raising a forefinger*]
For what has happened cannot be undone
although that might be wished by everyone
        [*pointing to* CORDAY]
We tried restraining her with peaceful sleep
and with the claims of a passion still more deep
Simonne as well as best she could she tried
        [*pointing to* SIMONNE]
but this girl here
        [*points to* CORDAY]
would not be turned aside
That man is now forgotten and we can
        [*points to* DUPERRET, *who moves back-
        wards on his knees from the dais*]
do nothing more Corday is focussed on this
        man
        [*points to* MARAT]

MARAT:   No
        [*raising himself high*]
I am right
and I will say it once more
Simonne
where is Bas
It is urgent
my call
        [SIMONNE *moves aside, stops still and
        stares bewitched at* CORDAY.]

SADE:   [*approaches the bath*]
Marat
what are all your pamphlets and speeches
compared with her
she stands there and will come to you
to kiss you and embrace you
Marat

an untouched virgin stands before you and
offers herself to you
See how she smiles
[CORDAY *stands erect and smiling, throw-*
*ing her hair aside. She has her hand on*
*the neckcloth in the place where the dag-*
*ger is hidden.*]
how her teeth shine
how she shakes her auburn hair aside
Marat
forget the rest
there's nothing else
beyond the body
Look
she stands there
her breast naked under the thin cloth
and perhaps she carries a knife
to intensify the love-play
[CORDAY *moves a step closer to the bath,*
*swaying lightly.* SIMONNE *stands frozen,*
*mechanically wringing the cloth in her*
*hands.*]

MARAT: Simonne Simonne
who was knocking at the door
SADE: A maiden
from the rural desert of a convent
Imagine
those pure girls lying on hard floors
in rough shifts
and the heated air from the fields
forcing its way to them through the barred
windows
Imagine
them lying there
with moist thighs and breasts

dreaming of those
who control life in the outside world
> [*The* FOUR SINGERS *come forward and
> begin a copulation mime.*
> ROSSIGNOL *mounts the strongest of her
> companions and performs acrobatics with
> them.*]

SADE: [*to musical accompaniment*]
And then she was tired of her isolation
and stirred up by the new age
and gathered up in the great tide
and wanted to be part of the Revolution
And what's the point of a revolution
without general copulation

CHORUS: And what's the point of a revolution
without general
copulation copulation copulation
> [*continues as a round. Mime ends.*]

SADE: Marat
as I sat there in the Bastille
for thirteen long years
I learned
that this is a world of bodies
each body pulsing with a terrible power
each body alone and racked with its own unrest
In that loneliness
marooned in a stone sea
I heard lips whispering continually
and felt all the time
in the palms of my hands and in my skin
touching and stroking
Shut behind thirteen bolted doors
my feet fettered
I dreamed only

of the orifices of the body
put there
so one may hook and twine oneself in them
> [A Patient *comes forward on tip-toe*
> *and stops behind the arena, listening*
> *tensely. Other* Patients *follow.*]

Continually I dreamed of this confrontation
and it was a dream of the most savage jealous
and cruellest imagining
Marat
these cells of the inner self
are worse than the deepest stone dungeon
and as long as they are locked
all your revolution remains
only a prison mutiny
to be put down
by corrupted fellow-prisoners

Chorus:    [*repeating with musical accompaniment*]
And what's the point of a revolution
without general copulation
> [*Music ends.*]

Corday:    [*to* Simonne. *Lute accompaniment.*]
Have you given my letter to Marat
Let me in it is vital
I must tell him what's happening in Caen
where they are gathering to destroy him

Marat:     Who's at the door
Simonne:   The girl from Caen
Marat:     Let her come in
> [Simonne *stands aside, shaking her head*
> *vigorously. She squats down at the edge*
> *of the dais behind the bath and hides her*
> *head in her hands.* Corday *moves to-*
> *wards the bath, swaying and smiling. Her*
> *hand still rests on her neckcloth.* Sade

**93**

*leaves the arena and goes to his dais,*
*where he remains, standing, watching*
*tensely.*]

CORDAY: [*softly*]
Marat
I will tell you the names of my heroes
but I am not betraying them
for I am speaking to a dead man

MARAT: [*raising himself up*]
Speak more clearly
I can't understand you
Come closer

CORDAY: [*coming closer to the bath with a fixed smile,*
*her body slowly swaying. She pushes a hand*
*under her neckcloth.*]
I name you names
Marat
the names of those
who have gathered at Caen
[*falling into a sing-song*]
I name Barbaroux
and Buzot
and Pétion
and Louvet
[*as she speaks the names her face is dis-*
*torted increasingly by an expression of*
*hate and lust*]
and Brissot
and Vergniaud
and Guadet
and Gensonné

MARAT: Who are you
Come closer
[MARAT *raises himself up high. The cloth*
*falls from his shoulders.* CORDAY *moves*

> *closer to him, swaying. Her left hand is*
> *stretched out as if to caress. In the right*
> *hand she holds the dagger under the neck-*
> *cloth.]*

CORDAY: [*humming words which sound like caresses*]
I am coming Marat
You cannot see me Marat
because you are dead

MARAT: [*crying out, raising himself up high, half-*
*naked*]
Bas
Take this down
Saturday the thirteenth of July seventeen hun-
dred and ninety three
A call to the people of France

> [CORDAY *stands immediately before* MA-
> RAT. *She moves her left hand close to his*
> *skin over his chest, his shoulders, his*
> *neck.* MARAT *sits arched over the back of*
> *the bath, a pen still in his hand.* CORDAY
> *pulls the dagger from her neckcloth. She*
> *holds it with both hands and raises her*
> *arms high to strike.*
> *The* HERALD *blows shrilly on his whistle.*
> *All players remain unmoving in their*
> *positions.*
> CORDAY *sinks back into herself.* MARAT
> *sits quietly, leaning forward.*]

## 31. INTERRUPTUS

HERALD: Now it's a part of Sade's dramatic plan
to interrupt the climax so this man
Marat can hear and gasp with his last breath
at how the world will go after his death

With a musical history we'll bring him up to
    date
From seventeen-ninety-three to eighteen-eight
        [*Music starts with very quick military
        march. The* FOUR SINGERS *sing and per-
        form grotesquely in time to the music.
        The* HERALD *displays banners showing
        the date of the events as they are de-
        scribed.*]

FOUR          Now your enemies fall*
SINGERS:      We're beheading them all [1793]
              Duperret
              and Corday
              executed in the same old way
              Robespierre has to get on [1794]
              he gets rid of Danton
              That was spring
              comes July
              and old Robespierre has to die
              Three rebellions a year [1795]
              but we're still of good cheer
              Malcontents
              all have been
              taught their lesson by the guillotine
              There's a shortage of wheat [1796]
              We're too happy to eat
              Austria
              cracks and then
              she surrenders to our men

              Fifteen glorious years
              Fifteen glorious years
              Years of peace
              years of war

* A literal verse translation of this section appears on page 103.

each year greater
than the year before
Marat
we're marching on

What brave soldiers we've got [1797]
Now the traitors are shot
Generals
boldly take
power in Paris
for the people's sake
Egypt's beaten down flat [1798]
Bonaparte did that
Cheer him as
they retreat
even though we lose our fleet
Bonaparte comes back [1799]
gives our rulers the sack
He's the man [1800]
brave and true
Bonaparte would die for you
Europe's free of her chains [1801]
Only England remains
but we want [1802]
wars to cease
so there's fourteen months of peace

[PATIENTS *join in, marching on the spot*]
Fifteen glorious years
Fifteen glorious years
Years of peace
years of war
each year greater
than the year before
Marat
we're marching on

England must be insane [1803]
wants to fight us again
so we march
off to war
Bonaparte is our Emperor [1804]
Nelson bothers our fleet
but he's shot off his feet
We're on top
yes we are
and we spit on Trafalgar
Now the Prussians retreat [1806]
Russia faces defeat [1807]
All the world
bends its knee
to Napoleon
and his family
Fight on land and on sea [1808]
All men want to be free
If they don't
never mind
we'll abolish all mankind

Fifteen glorious years
Fifteen glorious years
Years of peace
years of war
each year greater
than the one before
Marat
we're marching on
behind Napoleon

32.  THE  MURDER

> [*The entire cast have resumed their posi-
> tions exactly as before the song.*

CORDAY *clasps the knife with both hands above her head. Very slowly she lowers it towards* MARAT. SADE *follows her movements precisely, bending from the waist. She kills* MARAT.
PATIENTS *let out one single scream.*
CORDAY *crumples on the stage.*
SADE *stands contemplating the scene.*
MARAT *hangs as in David's classical picture, with his right hand over the edge of the bath. In his right hand he still holds his pen, in his left his papers.*]

## 33. EPILOGUE

[*The* ORCHESTRA *starts to play soft ceremonious music.*
*The* SISTERS *come forward and take charge of* CORDAY.
MARAT *steps out of his bath.*
COULMIER *comes forward.*]

COULMIER: Enlightened ladies pious gentlemen
let's close the history book and then
return to eighteen-eight the present day
of which though not unclouded we may say
it promises that mankind soon will cease
to fear the storms of war the squalls of peace
[*The music turns more and more into a monotonous march.*
*The* PATIENTS *in the background mark time. Their unrest increases.*]
For today we live in far different times
We have no oppressors no violent crimes
and although we're at war anyone can see
it can only end in victory

FOUR
SINGERS:
And if most have a little and few have a lot
you can see how much nearer our goal we
have got
We can say what we like without favour or
fear
and what we can't say we can breathe in your
ear

ROUX:
[*through the singing*]
When will you learn to see
When will you learn to take sides
When will you show them

FOUR
SINGERS:
And though we're locked up we're no longer
enslaved
and the honour of France is eternally saved
The useless debate the political brawl
are over there's one man to speak for us all
For he helps us in sickness and destitution
he's the leader who ended the Revolution
and everyone knows why we're cheering for
Napoleon our mighty Emperor

[*During the song* COULMIER *and his
family have congratulated* SADE *and chat-
ted with him.* SADE *presents various members of the cast. At this point the music
grows louder. The column of* PATIENTS
*begins to march forward.* SISTERS *and*
NURSES *try to restrain it. Several times the
column advances four paces and takes
three paces back. The music and marching rhythm grow in power.*
COULMIER *moves anxiously to the side
gesticulating.*]

ALL:
Led by him our soldiers go
over deserts and through the snow
A victory here and a victory there

Invincible glorious always victorious
for the good of all people everywhere
> [*The column advances still further,
> stamping some paces forward and some
> back. The* HERALD *begins to throw buck-
> ets etc. around.* NURSES *try to restrain
> him.* COULMIER's *family flee, screaming
> and shouting.*]

ALL:
> [*in confused but rhythmic shouts in time to
> the marching*]

Charenton Charenton
Napoleon Napoleon
Nation Nation
Revolution Revolution
Copulation Copulation
> [*The shouting grows. The column reaches
> the front. The struggle between* NURSES
> *and* HERALD *develops and catches the at-
> tention of the others. Suddenly the
> whole stage is fighting.*
>
> SADE *watches with a faint smile, almost
> indulgent.*
>
> *The actors have moved to the side.*
>
> *Music, shouting and tramping increase to
> a tempest.*
>
> *A strong wind blows in through the up-
> per side windows. The huge curtains bil-
> low far into the room.*
>
> *The* NURSES *go among the patients wield-
> ing their batons.*
>
> ROUX *springs forward and places himself
> before the marchers, his back to them,
> still with fettered arms.*]

ROUX:
When will you learn to see
When will you learn to take sides

[*He tries to force them back, but is drawn in and vanishes from sight in the still advancing ranks.*

*The* PATIENTS *are fully at the mercy of their mad marchlike dance. Many of them hop and spin in ecstasy.*

COULMIER *incites the* NURSES *to extreme violence.*

PATIENTS *are struck down.*

*The* HERALD *is now in front of the orchestra, leaping about in time to the music.*

SADE *stands upright on his chair, laughing triumphantly.*

*In desperation* COULMIER *gives the signal to close the curtain.*]

CURTAIN

## LITERAL VERSE TRANSLATION
## OF THE ORIGINAL TEXT *

In the Vendée the battle rages
with deeds both cruel and courageous
between our men and the king's supporters
and we drive them from their quarters
With flying banners we march along
an avenging army with fire and song
called Regiment Marat in your renown
and with it we mow our enemies down
Marat the things you bade us do
we now with all our strength put through
Our foes lie beaten in the sand
or take their lives with their own hand
And with cannon and horse we march along
and storm the counter-revolutionary throng
in Lyon where for example's sake
we send three thousand to the stake
And now through Nantes our army passes
where we drown citizens in masses
and every house where a rebel is found
we raze relentlessly to the ground
And at last with flying banners we come
to the traitor city of Toulon
and with us is one whose star is ascending
who can lead us on to victories unending
You see Marat how we advance
and now we begin to thin our own ranks
Just as you told us so must above all
the weak and incapable go to the wall
Robespierre puts Danton to the axe

* Page 96.

and sends in his wake with all despatch
many of our old confederates
on whom in our ignorance we'd based our hopes
Marat we cannot believe it's true
what our new bosses start to do
Beside the nobles we see in the carts
Jacobins who were once dear to our hearts
and the axe treats them all regardless of name
and when they are corpses they look all the same
Marat we can only stand and gape
at the curious moods of fate
Now we see Robespierre bound and trussed
and already his head has rolled in the dust
Marat how does this all fit together
that the one lot always condemns the other
Tell us Marat must it be so
that someone above for the sake of show
must always direct and always lead
and in the doing it forfeit his head
Marat to comfort you we can say
whom we now have with us today
Napoleon Bonaparte now stands there
like you comes from Corsica or Sardinia
and he has promised us peace eternal
and gives us work in the arsenal
and in honour of the revolution
he calls himself emperor Napoleon
It is we can tell you a feast for the eye
and with rumbling bellies we watch it go by
We just stand and stare
and the holy men bless us in prayer

## AUTHOR'S NOTE ON THE HISTORICAL
## BACKGROUND TO THE PLAY

Even before his confinement in the stronghold of Vincennes
and the Paris Bastille Sade had produced plays in his residence
La Coste. During the thirteen years of his imprisonment,
between the ages of 33 and 46, he wrote seventeen plays in
addition to his large prose works. In later years he brought out
a further dozen tragedies, comedies, operas, pantomimes and
one-acters in verse. Out of all these pieces only one, *Oxstiern
ou les malheurs du libertinage,* was performed in a public
theatre during his years of liberty 1790–1801—and taken off
at once after a scandal.

From 1801 until his death in 1814 Sade was interned in the
asylum of Charenton, where over a period of years he had
the chance of producing plays among the patients and appear-
ing as an actor himself. Charenton (to follow J. L. Casper's
description in his *Charakteristik der französischen Medizin,*
published in 1822 in Leipzig) was an institution which catered
for all whose behaviour had made them socially impossible,
whether they were lunatics or not. Here were locked up
'perpetrators of crimes whose handling in open court would
not be in the public interest, as well as others who had been
arrested for serious political misdemeanours or who had allowed themselves to be used as the evil tools of high intrigues.'

In exclusive Paris circles it was considered a rare pleasure to
attend Sade's theatrical performances in the 'hiding-place for
the moral rejects of civilised society.' It is of course probable
that these amateur performances consisted in the main of
declamatory pieces in the prevailing style: the bulk of Sade's
dramatic work does not reach up to the boldness and con-
sistency of his prose. But in his *Dialogue entre un prêtre et*

*un moribund* and above all in *La philosophie dans le boudoir* there are analytical and philosophical conversations, carried out against a background of bodily excess, which clearly show his dramatic perception. His visual mode of thought is also seen again and again in the exceptionally realistic descriptive passages of the novels.

Sade's encounter with Marat, which is the subject of this play, is entirely imaginary, based only on the single fact that it was Sade who spoke the memorial address at Marat's funeral. Even in this speech his real attitude towards Marat is questionable, since he made the speech primarily to save his own skin; at that time his position was in danger, his name on the list of those marked out for the guillotine.

What interests me in bringing together Sade and Marat is the conflict between an individualism carried to extreme lengths and the idea of a political and social upheaval. Even Sade knew the Revolution to be necessary: his works are one single attack on a corrupt ruling class. He flinched however from the violent methods of the progressives and, like the modern advocate of a third approach, fell between two stools. He did indeed, on his release from prison in 1790, place himself at the service of the National Assembly and became an official in the *Section des Piques*, where he was put in charge of hospitals. He was even made a judge. But the long years of imprisonment had left their mark on him: he remained an outsider and found contact with his fellow men difficult.

His claim that he had suffered at the hands of the old regime cannot be taken as evidence of heroism, since his imprisonment was due to charges of sexual extravagance and not to political acts. These excesses, in monstrous written form, were once again to cause his downfall under the new regime.

Sade's own picture of himself as a rebel can be seen in a letter written from prison to his wife in 1783, in which he says:

'You say that one cannot approve my mode of thought. What does that signify? Anyone who imagines he can prescribe a mode of thought to another must be quite out of his senses. My mode of thought is the result of my own reflections, it is a part of my life, of my own nature. It is not in my power to alter it, and if it were in my power I should not do it. This mode of thought which you condemn is the only comfort of my life: it relieves all my sufferings in prison, it provides all my pleasure in this world; it means more to me than my own life. It is not my mode of thought that has caused my misfortunes, but the mode of thought of others.'

It is difficult to imagine Sade in the role of a worker for the common good. He felt himself obliged to adopt a double-faced attitude. On the one hand he approved Marat's radical arguments, on the other he saw the dangers of totalitarianism. His views on the fair division of worldly goods did not go to the length that he could contemplate giving up his own house and property, and he did not submit tamely when forced to give up La Coste after it had been plundered and burnt.

Sade's plays represent his last attempt to communicate with his fellow beings, but with advancing age he relapsed entirely into solitariness. A doctor at Charenton wrote, 'I frequently encountered him as he walked alone, with heavy dragging steps, very negligently dressed, through the corridors near his home. I never saw him speak with anybody. I would greet him as I passed by and he would return my greeting with a cold politeness that precluded any thought of conversation.'

If the idea of bringing Sade into contact with Marat in his final hour is my own invention, the picture of Marat at this time accords with fact. The psychosomatic skin disease from which he suffered in the last years of his life—a legacy of privation in the cellars in which he hid—forced him to spend many hours in the bath in order to soothe his itching. And here he was on Saturday, 13 July 1793, when Charlotte Corday came three times to his door before she gained entry and stabbed him.

Marat's words in the play correspond in content and often

almost exactly in expression with the writings he left behind. What is said about the various phases of his life is also authentic. He left home at the age of sixteen, studied medicine, lived for some years in England, was renowned as a physician, misunderstood as a scientist, won social honours. Subsequently, however, after subjecting society to the shafts of his criticism, he placed himself entirely in the service of the Revolution and, on account of his violent and uncompromising character, was made the scapegoat for many acts of cruelty.

It was not until the beginning of the present century that writers like Rosbroy, Bax and Gottschalk began to revise the usual one-sided view of Marat and to draw attention to the acuteness of his political and scientific arguments. Scarcely any other personality of the French Revolution has been depicted in so revolting and bloodthirsty a light by the bourgeois historians of the nineteenth century as Marat. This is not really surprising, since his ideas lead in a direct line to Marxism, though they also come perilously near to the idea of dictatorship, even when he himself protested, 'Dictator: the word must be abolished. I hate anything to do with masters and slaves.'

From our vantage point today we must bear in mind that Marat was one of those who were in the process of building the socialist image, and that much in his ideas of change by forceful means was still undigested or overreached itself. Beside him in the play I have placed the former priest Jacques Roux, who surpassed Marat in his rabble-rousing and passionate pacifism. I have ignored the fact that Marat in the last days of his life turned away from Roux and, perhaps in an attack of persecution mania, disowned him. Roux, one of the most fascinating personalities of the Revolution, is here given the function of a champion and perfectionist, an *alter ego* against whom Marat's ideas can be measured.

I have also taken liberties in the portrayal of Duperret, the Girondist deputy. Here he is shown as the conservative patriot, one of many thousands of similar sort. He is also pressed into service as Charlotte Corday's lover, a role held in reality by a M. Tournelis, who left Caen to join the royalist refugees in Koblenz. In leaving him out of account I have acted entirely in the spirit of the Revolution itself, in the confusion of which no one was very exact in the matter of accusations and recriminations: poor Duperret himself, for instance, to whom Charlotte Corday has been recommended by the rebel group in Caen, had to pay for their brief encounter with his head.

Charlotte Corday had in fact let nobody into her secret. Schooled by convent life in the art of ecstatic withdrawal, she went her way alone and, with thoughts of Joan of Arc and the biblical Judith in mind, made a saint out of herself.

PETER WEISS

MUSIC COMPOSED SPECIALLY FOR
THE FIRST BRITISH PRODUCTION OF THE PLAY
BY R. C. PEASLEE

*Copyright © 1965 by Richard Peaslee*
*All rights reserved*
*The full score and permission to use the music*
*may be obtained from Galaxy Music Corporation,*
*2121 Broadway, New York, N.Y.*

**HOMAGE TO MARAT**

LIVELY ♩=120-128

FOUR YEARS AF-TER THE RE-VO-LU-TION AND THE OLD KING'S EX-E-CU-TION

FOUR YEARS AF-TER RE RE-MEM-BER HOW THOSE COURT-I-ERS TOOK THEIR FI-NAL BOW

CHORUS

STRING UP EV'-RY — A-RIS-TO-CRAT

OUT WITH THE PRIESTS LET THEM LIVE ON THEIR FAT

ETC.

**MARAT WE'RE POOR**

BROAD ♩=84-88

MA-RAT WE'RE POOR — AND THE POOR STAY POOR — MA-RAT DON'T

MAKE — US WAIT AN-Y — MORE GIVE US OUR RIGHTS AND WE DON'T CARE

(SHOUTED)

HOW — WE WANT — OUR RE-VOL-U-TION NOW

CORDAY WALTZ

MODERATELY FAST ♩ = 140

ONCE BOTH — OF US SAW THE WORLD — MUST GO — AND

CHANGE AS WE READ — IN GREAT — ROUS-SEAU BUT CHANGE — MEANT

ONE THING TO YOU — I SEE — AND SOME-THING QUITE DIF-FRENT TO

ME — THE VER-Y SAME WORDS— WE BOTH— HAVE

SAID — TO GIVE OUR I — DEALS — WINGS TO SPREAD— BUT

MY WAY WAS TRUE — WHILE FOR YOU — THE HIGH-WAY LEAD

O - VER MOUN - TAINS OF DEAD — ETC.

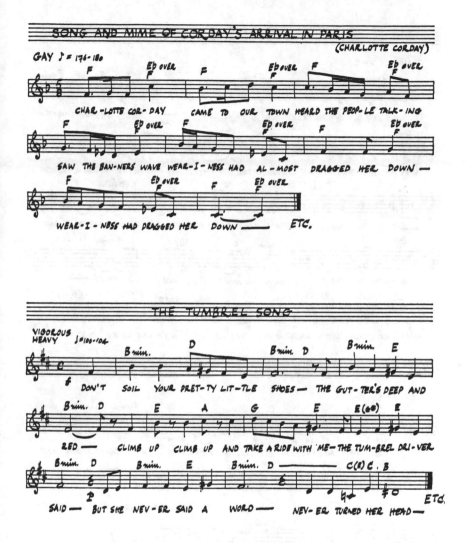

SONG AND MIME OF CORDAY'S ARRIVAL IN PARIS

(CHARLOTTE CORDAY)

GAY ♩ = 176-180

CHAR-LOTTE COR-DAY CAME TO OUR TOWN HEARD THE PEOP-LE TALK-ING

SAW THE BAN-NERS WAVE WEAR-I-NESS HAD AL-MOST DRAGGED HER DOWN —

WEAR-I-NESS HAD DRAGGED HER DOWN — ETC.

THE TUMBREL SONG

VIGOROUS
HEAVY ♩=100-104

DON'T SOIL YOUR PRET-TY LIT-TLE SHOES — THE GUT-TER'S DEEP AND

RED — CLIMB UP CLIMB UP AND TAKE A RIDE WITH ME — THE TUM-BREL DRI-VER

SAID — BUT SHE NEV-ER SAID A WORD — NEV-ER TURNED HER HEAD —

113

THE PEOPLE'S REACTION

FAST MARCH ♩=128

WHY HAVE THEY GOT THE CASH   WHY HAVE THEY GOT THE POW-ER   WHY-WHY-WHY-WHY

WHY — HAVE THEY GOT THE FRIENDS AT THE TOP —   WHY HAVE THEY GOT THE JOBS AT THE TOP —

WE'VE GOT NOTH-ING — AL-WAYS HAD NOTH-ING NOTH-ING BUT HOLES AND

MIL-LIONS OF THEM   LIV-ING IN HOLES   DY-ING IN HOLES —

HOLES IN OUR BEL-LIES AND   HOLES IN OUR CLOTHES   MA-RAT WE'RE POOR —   ETC.

THOSE FAT MONKEYS

LIVELY ♩=156-160

THOSE FAT MON-KEYS — COV-ERED IN BANK-NOTES   HAVE CHAM-PAGNE AND

BRAN-DY ON TAP —   THEY'RE UP TO THEIR EYE-BALLS IN FRANC-NOTES

WE'RE UP TO OUR   NOS-ES IN CRAP   ETC.

114

## ONE DAY IT WILL COME TO PASS

MODERATELY SLOW ♩=120-128

Emin. Amin. Emin. B Amin.⁶

ONE DAY IT WILL COME TO PASS MAN WILL LIVE IN HAR-MO-NY

Emin. C Amin. B sus. B Emin.

WITH HIM-SELF AND WITH HIS FEL-LOW MAN ____ ETC.

## POOR MARAT IN YOUR BATHTUB SEAT

ALLEGRETTO ♩=100-104

Bb Eb F Bb Gmin. Dmin.

POOR MA - RAT IN YOUR BATH-TUB SEAT YOUR LIFE ON THIS PLAN-ET IS

C F Eb Cmin. F Gmin. D⁷

NEAR COM - PLETE CLOS-ER AND CLOS-ER TO YOU DEATH CREEPS THOUGH

Gmin. Bb(D) Eb F Bb

THERE ON HER BENCH CHAR-LOTTE COR - DAY SLEEPS ETC.

## COPULATION ROUND

GAY ♩=120-128

AND WHAT'S THE POINT OF A REV-O-LU-TION WITH-OUT GEN-ER-AL

GEN-ER-AL COP-U-LA-TION COP-U-LA-TION COP-U-LA-TION AND

116

CONCORDIA UNIVERSITY LIBRARY

3 9371 00054 6531

PT 2685.E5 V43 1981
Weiss, Peter
Persecution and
PETE Assassination of Jean-Paul

Peter Weiss, painter, film director, novelist and playwright, was born at Nowawes, near Berlin, in 1916. He left Germany when Nazism came in, and has lived in Sweden ever since, although he continues to write in German.

His experimental films have been shown in this country, and one of his novels, *Leavetaking*, has been translated.

This play opened in Berlin at the Schillertheater, in April 1964 and evoked an extraordinary response from the press as well as the audiences: throughout the reviews Peter Weiss was mentioned as the German playwright to succeed Brecht, having brought a new concept of theater to the international scene. When Peter Brook's production was performed in England by the Royal Shakespeare Company a little later that year, it was greeted with similar acclaim.

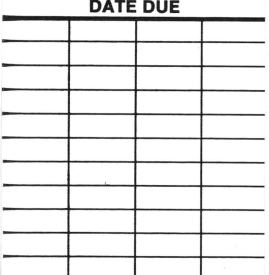

**DATE DUE**